The best interests of the child – A dialogue between theory and practice

Council of Europe

Cover and layout: Document and Publications
Production Department (SPDP), Council of Europe
Cover Photo: Shutterstock

Council of Europe Publishing
F-67075 Strasbourg Cedex
http://book.coe.int

Edited by Milka Sormunen
ISBN 978-92-871-8252-4
© Council of Europe, March 2016
Printed at the Council of Europe

Contents

Introduction

Everyone has heard about it, but we do not actually know what it means – or do we? The concept of the best interests of the child is essential, yet vague and indeterminate. It has existed for a long time, but its importance grew when it was included in the United Nations Convention on the Rights of the Child (UNCRC).[1] Article 3.1 of the UNCRC states that:

> [i]n all actions concerning children, whether undertaken by public or private social welfare institutions, courts of law, administrative authorities or legislative bodies, the best interests of the child shall be a primary consideration.

What does this mean in practice? How should the concept be interpreted and applied?

The Belgian authorities and the Council of Europe wished to emphasise the role of the best interests of the child and further develop the normative provisions concerning this concept, specifically the deontological, ethical and procedural rules related to it. The European Conference on the Best Interests of the Child, "a dialogue between theory and practice", was thus organised within the framework of the Belgian Chairmanship of the Committee of Ministers of the Council of Europe in collaboration with the Council of Europe Children's Rights Division in Brussels on 9 and 10 December 2014, linking the 25th anniversary of the UNCRC with the Human Rights Day.

The conference was one of the priorities set by the Belgian Chairmanship under the topic "Promotion and realisation of human rights". The aim of the conference was to shed light on a vague, indeterminate, yet very central concept whose importance for children's rights is unquestionable. By organising the conference, we wanted to initiate and encourage discussion in order to spread knowledge and enhance understanding of the concept of the child's best interests.

Clarifying the concept of the best interests of the child and its implementation in practice is important for children's human rights in general. One of the main challenges related to the best interests of the child is to mobilise decision makers around the concept so that it is genuinely seen as a primary consideration in their daily work. Judges, medical professionals, psychosocial workers, psychologists, educators and other professionals who work with children and youth must have the necessary tools at their disposal to assess and determine the child's interests. They must also

---

1. The UN Convention on the Rights of the Child was adopted and opened for signature, ratification and accession by General Assembly Resolution 44/25 of 20 November 1989. It entered into force 2 September 1990, in accordance with Article 49.

understand the concept of the child's best interests in order to make good decisions that respect their human rights.

The conference explored the challenges decision makers face when working to implement the best interests of the child. The target group of the conference included experts, policy makers and practitioners involved in decisions that have an impact on children's lives, as well as representatives of the major European institutions and non-governmental organisations protecting the rights of the child. Each member state of the Council of Europe was invited to send a delegation of two participants to the conference. For Belgium, as well as for the Council of Europe, it was essential that all partners, experts, decision makers and practitioners, but also children, had the chance to express their views and contribute to the discussion. Organising the conference was a way to bring together a diverse range of actors and combine theory and practice in an effective way.

This publication reflects the main ideas discussed in the conference and sheds light on different aspects of the concept of the best interests of the child. In so doing, it presents 21 texts that all offer their own viewpoint on the concept. Together, these texts provide a comprehensive view of the best interests of the child, wherein the different dimensions of the concept are articulated.

This publication is structured into four chapters discussing the best interest of the child from different points of view.

The first chapter introduces general reflections on the best interests of the child that will help in understanding the regulatory framework surrounding the concept and its application. Jorge Cardona Llorens, member of the UN Committee on the Rights of the Child, discusses the strengths and limitations of the committee's General Comment No. 14 on the right of the child to have his or her best interests taken as a primary consideration. Nigel Cantwell offers a critical point of view and discusses whether the concept offers added value to children's human rights. Olga Khazova, also a member of the UN Committee on the Rights of the Child, discusses questions related to the legal framework where the concept applies. Gerison Lansdown analyses the connection between the best interests of the child and participation, and Jacques Fierens introduces an idea of the best interests of the child as a guiding light, rather like the North Star. A study by the Children's Rights Knowledge Centre (KeKi) on children's best interests is also presented by Eveline van Hooijdonk.

The second chapter focuses on the process of assessing, determining and monitoring the best interests of the child. What tools can we use to evaluate, determine and apply the concept of the best interests of the child? How can we involve the child in the process in order to fully respect the requirements of the UNCRC? Urszula Markowska-Manista discusses marginalised children and the legacy of Janusz Korczak. Margrite Kalverboer introduces a model for the best interests of the child as a tool that can be helpful in practical situations, and Carla van Os discusses that model in the context of recently arrived refugee children. Hanne Op de Beeck asks whether systems developed for return decisions could serve as an inspiration when developing other monitoring systems.

The third chapter sheds light on the workability of such an indeterminate concept as the best interests of the child, in practice, in different environments. Regína Jensdóttir, Head of the Children's Rights Division of the Council of Europe discusses the concept of the best interests from the perspective of the Council of Europe. The European Commission Coordinator for the rights of the child, Margaret Tuite, discusses the role of this concept in the work of the European Union, and Tam Baillie, Scotland's Commissioner for Children and Young People, presents the perspective of an ombudsperson. Johanna Nyman, President of the European Youth Forum, analyses the concept from the perspective of young people and their rights. Bernard De Vos, Ombudsman for Children's Rights of the Federation Wallonia-Brussels, Belgium, discusses conditions for decision making that respects the rights of the child, as well as his past experiences as an ombudsman. Jana Hainsworth, Secretary General of Eurochild, discusses the child's best interests and challenges to its implementation from the point of view of civil society.

The fourth chapter focuses on the best interests of the child in family affairs, a central theme of the conference. Aida Grgić, lawyer at the European Court of Human Rights, analyses the best interests of the child in the case law of the European Court of Human Rights related to family affairs. Cristina Martins, President of International Federation of Social Workers Europe (IFSW), discusses best interests in the context of social work, and Valeriu Ghilețchi, Chair of the Social Affairs Committee of the Parliamentary Assembly of the Council of Europe, presents problems that arise when separating children from their families. Astrid Hirschelmann presents research on children whose parents are in prison, and Géraldine Mathieu discusses best interests in the context of the right to know one's origins.

Finally, the Appendices in this publication offer the full text of the speeches given by three Belgian ministers and the Head of the Council of Europe Liaison Officer to the European Union, followed by the conclusions of the conference, and the Executive summaries of the contributions to the conference.

History has shown that periods of economic, financial, social and environmental crisis do not favour children and youth, or the defence and promotion of their rights. Yet, it is in these times more than any other that children must remain at the heart of decision makers' concerns. Whether we admit it or not, the concept of the best interests of the child is one of the most central in the field of children's rights. Whether we like the concept or not, it is an essential provision in a binding international convention and has to be taken into account. If we want to understand children's rights, we cannot neglect to give particular attention to the concept of the best interests of the child.

We hope you find this publication interesting and that it succeeds in continuing the dialogue between theory and practice that shaped the conference in such a fruitful way.

Belgium   *Council of Europe*

Chapter 1

The concept of the best interests of the child: general reflections

Presentation of General Comment No. 14: strengths and limitations, points of consensus and dissent emerging in its drafting

Jorge Cardona Llorens
Professor of Public International Law, University of Valencia, Member of the Committee on the Rights of the Child[2]

Writing about the child's best interests is a comparatively easy task for me because I have already made presentations in numerous conferences pertaining to General Comment No. 14 of the UN Committee on the Rights of the Child. But this time, the challenge is quite different; the purpose of this text is to present current questions and concerns relating to the concept of the child's best interests and its interpretation by the Committee on the Rights of the Child in General Comment No. 14. In this article, I try to identify the strengths and weaknesses of the General Comment, the points of consensus and dissent which emerged in its drafting, and the difficulties of tangibly fulfilling the child's best interests in the decision-making process.

This is not an easy task, because I must uphold the confidentiality of the deliberations in the Committee, and because what I normally try to do is to emphasise the strong points of the General Comment and the benefits of its implementation, not the weak points.

I have decided to concentrate on four questions: firstly the child's best interests as an indeterminate but not discretionary legal concept, secondly the problems of assessing and determining children's best interests in the adoption of general measures, thirdly the relationship between the child's best interests and the other legitimate interests involved and lastly the consequences of maintaining the threefold legal nature of the child's best interests as a right, a legal principle and a procedural rule.

---

2. This text expresses the author's opinion and not necessarily the opinion of the United Nations Committee on the Rights of the Child.

The child's best interests as an indeterminate but not discretionary legal concept

Firstly I shall concentrate on the child's best interests as an indeterminate but not discretionary legal concept. When I joined the Committee in 2011, the chairperson asked me to choose the working groups to which I wished to belong. I chose three: the working group on the child's best interests, the working group on state obligations regarding the impact of the business sector on children's rights and the group on reform of the Committee's working methods. In principle, the last two were to begin their work in 2011 and the first, on best interests, was in the process of finishing its work.

The chairperson gave me the text which the Committee had already drawn up and asked me my frank opinion. After a first reading, and because frankness had been requested of me, I said that I disliked the text. "Why?" the chairperson enquired. "Because on reading the document I find no criteria for assessing and determining a child's interest in a given situation," was my reply. Having heard my answer, the chairperson said to me, "Very well, Jorge. Your opinion coincides with several which we have received in the last few weeks. Since you are the newcomer to the working group, you'll be the rapporteur for revising the text so that it answers the question you have raised."

What is the basic question? True, the concept of a child's best interests is adaptable to the situation of each child and to the evolution of knowledge about the child's development. But, as was emphasised in the General Comment, this flexibility:

> may also leave room for manipulation; the concept of the child's best interests has been abused by Governments and other State authorities to justify racist policies, for example; by parents to defend their own interests in custody disputes; by professionals who could not be bothered, and who dismiss the assessment of the child's best interests as irrelevant or unimportant.[3]

So this was my first besetting concern: the idea of a child's best interests is indeed an adaptable concept embracing various, constantly evolving questions, an indeterminate legal concept to be determined case by case. However, it should be clearly established that it is on no account a discretionary concept.

The sentence which I wrote at the top of my blackboard in my office was the following: For the same decision, the assessment and determination of the best interests of five different children should prompt us to make five different determinations (given that no two children are alike in the same circumstances and in the same situation). But the assessment and determination of one child's best interests made by five adults individually in the adoption of a decision should arrive at the same result.

In other words, although the child's best interests are an indeterminate legal concept, their assessment and determination should be founded on objective criteria. The concept is intended to ensure both the full and effective realisation of all rights secured by the United Nations Convention on the Rights of the Child (UNCRC), and the child's overall development. Accordingly, the child's best interests are not what I consider best for a child but what, objectively, secures for the child both the full and effective realisation

---

3. Committee on the Rights of the Child, General Comment No. 14 (2013) on the right of the child to have his or her best interests taken as a primary consideration (Article 3.1), paragraph 34.

of all the rights secured in the convention, and his or her overall development. This reasoning explains Part V of the General Comment entitled "Implementation: assessing and determining the child's best interests". The Committee was not content just to say that assessment of the child's best interests should always be a single operation to be performed in each specific case having regard to the circumstances specific to each child, but also tried to show the proper path for this.

That is where the problems begin! What circumstances must be taken into account? Which elements should be considered in assessing them? Which procedural safety nets should be provided for assessing and determining the child's best interests when decisions concerning him or her are taken?

The General Comment lists the circumstances, elements and safeguards which the Committee has decided to propose to states in every case. But, as explicitly stated in the General Comment, it is a:

> non-exhaustive and non-hierarchical list of elements that could be included in a best-interests assessment by any decision maker having to determine a child's best interests. The non-exhaustive nature of the elements in the list implies that it is possible to go beyond those and consider other factors relevant in the specific circumstances of the individual child or group of children. All the elements of the list must be taken into consideration and balanced in light of each situation. The list should provide concrete guidance, yet flexibility.[4]

Among the elements to be taken into account are the child's views; the child's identity; preservation of the family environment and maintaining family relations; the child's care, protection and safety; situations of vulnerability; the child's right to health or the child's right to education. In the Committee's opinion:

> the basic best-interests assessment is a general assessment of all relevant elements of the child's best interests, the weight of each element depending on the others. … The content of each element will necessarily vary from child to child and from case to case, depending on the type of decision and the concrete circumstances, as will the importance of each element in the overall assessment.[5]

Concerning balance between these different elements, the Committee has identified three situations to take into account:

a) Firstly, where the various elements taken into consideration for assessing best interests in a given case conflict with the circumstances peculiar to it (for example, concern to preserve the family environment conflicts with the imperative of protecting the child from the risk of violence or abuse by parents). That is, balance between the elements, circumstances and factors to be taken into account.

b) Secondly, the problems which arise when factors linked with concern to protect the child (possibly involving limitation or restriction of rights) need to be assessed in relation to measures of "empowerment" (which implies full exercise of rights without restriction). That is, balance between the child's protection and empowerment.

c) Thirdly, the connected question of the evolving character of the child's capacities and the need for decision makers to envisage measures which can be reviewed or adjusted accordingly rather than take final, irreversible decisions. And simultaneously,

---

4.   General Comment No. 14 (2013), paragraph 50.
5.   General Comment No. 14 (2013), paragraph 80.

the need to assess the continuity and stability of the child's present and future situation. That is, striking a balance between the child as an evolving subject and the need for the child to enjoy stability.

Balance firstly in selecting the relevant circumstances, elements and safeguards. Balance secondly between protection and empowerment. Balance thirdly in weighing up all the elements taken into consideration.

But I acknowledge that here we might find weak points: has the Committee actually struck these balances? Are the stated criteria sufficient?

Assessing and determining children's best interests when general measures are adopted

The second question I wish to address is the relationship between the child's best interests and children's best interests (individual and collective best interests): how do we assess and determine the child's best interests when adopting general measures.

The reader will have appreciated that on each occasion I have spoken of assessing and determining a child's best interests in connection with an individual decision. But Article 3.1 of the convention does not only speak of individual decisions. It sets out to ensure that the right in question is guaranteed in all decisions and actions which concern children. This means that in every decision concerning a child or children, the child's best interests must be an overriding consideration. The term "decision" is not construed purely as individual decisions but also as all acts, conduct, proposals, services, procedures and other measures. That is why there is question not only of the decisions of administrative bodies or courts, but also of legislative bodies.

But if we have said that no two children are alike, that one child's best interests differ from another's, how is it possible to assess and determine children's best interests generally? Moreover, concerning general implementing measures, what should be the procedure for ensuring that the child's best interests are a primary consideration in legislation and in the framing and execution of policies at all tiers of public authorities? Clearly we cannot use the same procedure as for an individual decision.

The Committee's final agreement in the matter was that it:

> demands a continuous process of child-rights impact assessment (CRIA) to predict the impact of any proposed law, policy or budgetary allocation on children and the enjoyment of their rights, and child-rights impact evaluation to evaluate the actual impact of implementation.[6]

> The child-rights impact assessment (CRIA) can predict the impact of any proposed policy, legislation, regulation, budget or other administrative decision which affect children and the enjoyment of their rights and should complement ongoing monitoring and evaluation of the impact of measures on children's rights. CRIA needs to be built into Government processes at all levels and as early as possible in the development of policy and other general measures in order to ensure good governance for children's rights.[7]

---

6.   General Comment No. 14 (2013), paragraph 35.
7.   General Comment No. 14 (2013), paragraph 99.

Naturally, the assertion that respect for the child's best interests in collective decisions requires states to make studies of the impact of all their decisions is not readily acceptable for states. However, and this is the second important point, is there another way? And at all events, does the impact study suffice to assess and determine children's best interests before the adoption of a general measure?

The relationship between the child's best interests and the other legitimate interests involved

The third question that I wish to emphasise is the relationship between the child's best interests and the other legitimate interests involved. There is a danger of conflict between children's best interests and the public interests, or the interests of other players. What criteria are to be applied in these situations? Here we come to a question which raised considerable debate in the drafting of the General Comment: the collision of the child's best interests with other interests.

Firstly it is important to ask whether the child's best interests should be "a" primary consideration or "the" primary consideration. I do not think it violates the confidentiality of the Committee's proceedings to say that this question was one of the most extensively discussed. Finally, as the General Comment says:

> the Committee recognizes the need for a degree of flexibility in its application. The best interests of the child – once assessed and determined – might conflict with other interests or rights (e.g. of other children, the public, parents, etc.). Potential conflicts between the best interests of a child, considered individually, and those of a group of children or children in general have to be resolved on a case-by-case basis, carefully balancing the interests of all parties and finding a suitable compromise. The same must be done if the rights of other persons are in conflict with the child's best interests. If harmonization is not possible, authorities and decision-makers will have to analyse and weigh the rights of all those concerned, bearing in mind that the right of the child to have his or her best interests taken as a primary consideration means that the child's interests have high priority and are not just one of several considerations. Therefore, a larger weight must be attached to what serves the child best.[8]

Of course these are fine words. But having read them, is it now clear how to resolve a conflict between the interest of the child and another interest?

Plainly, some situations are easier than others. For example, in matters of adoption (Article 21), the principle of the child's best interests is further strengthened; it is not to be simply "a primary consideration", but "the paramount consideration". The child's best interests must indeed be the decisive factor in decisions on adoption, but also in other areas. This is true of Article 9 – separation from parents; Article 10 – family reunification; Article 37.c – separation from adults in detention; and paragraph 2.b.iii of Article 40 – procedural guarantees, notably the parents' presence at hearings in criminal cases involving children in conflict with the law. In all these cases, the convention gives the child's best interests greater weight than other interests.

---

8.   General Comment No. 14 (2013), paragraph 39.

But there is a large number of other situations not provided for. The Committee has tried to propose certain reflections to settle the conflicts. Allow me to emphasise three of them:

a) Firstly, the child's best interests must be assessed in all circumstances. As indicated in the General Comment:

> The words "shall be" place a strong legal obligation on States and mean that States may not exercise discretion as to whether children's best interests are to be assessed and ascribed the proper weight as a primary consideration in any action undertaken.[9]

b) Secondly:

> The expression 'primary consideration' means that the child's best interests may not be considered on the same level as all other considerations. This strong position is justified by the special situation of the child: dependency, maturity, legal status and, often, voicelessness. Children have less possibility than adults to make a strong case for their own interests and those involved in decisions affecting them must be explicitly aware of their interests. If the interests of children are not highlighted, they tend to be overlooked.[10]

c) Thirdly:

> Viewing the best interests of the child as 'primary' requires a consciousness about the place that children's interests must occupy in all actions and a willingness to give priority to those interests in all circumstances, but especially when an action has an undeniable impact on the children concerned.[11]

In conclusion, where the child's best interests and other interests involved come into collision, the decision maker must carefully balance the interests of all parties by finding an acceptable compromise. If harmonisation is impossible, the authorities and persons responsible will need to analyse and weigh up the rights of all parties concerned, bearing in mind that the child's right to have his best interests treated as a primary consideration means that the child's interests rank high in priority and are not one consideration among others. In spite of everything, I must admit that, regarding this third question, the Committee does not give very exact criteria for adopting the decision. And the question which arises is whether it this even possible.

The consequences of maintaining the threefold legal nature of the child's best interests as a right, a legal principle and a procedural rule

My fourth and last question concerns the legal nature of the child's best interests. This question is discussed at the beginning of the General Comment which begins by saying that the child's best interests are a right, a principle and a rule of procedure. This definition is most important. The child's best interests have traditionally been seen as an interpretative legal principle: if a legal provision lends itself to several interpretations, the one most effectively serving the child's best interest should be chosen.

---

9. General Comment No. 14 (2013), paragraph 36.
10. General Comment No. 14 (2013), paragraph 37.
11. General Comment No. 14 (2013), paragraph 40.

But the child's best interests are not only a legal principle, they are fundamentally a subjective right. The child has the right to have his or her best interests assessed and made a primary consideration when various different interests are examined in order to reach a decision on the question at issue. This right will be applied in all decision making concerning a child, a specified or unspecified group of children or children in general. It is a self-executing right too, so it may be invoked before a court. This question accounts for the last-minute change of title for the General Comment. The title for the General Comment is not "the principle of the child's best interests", but "the right of the child to have his or her interests taken as a primary consideration".

However, to be able to demand respect for this right, the holder of the right (or his or her representative) must know what were the factors, elements and circumstances assessed by the decision maker. This logically brings us to the third attribute of the concept of the child's best interests, as a procedural rule:

> Whenever a decision is to be made that will affect a specific child, an identified group of children or children in general, the decision-making process must include an evaluation of the possible impact (positive or negative) of the decision on the child or children concerned. Assessing and determining the best interests of the child require procedural guarantees. Furthermore, the justification of a decision must show that the right has been explicitly taken into account. In this regard, States parties shall explain how the right has been respected in the decision, that is, what has been considered to be in the child's best interests; what criteria it is based on; and how the child's interests have been weighed against other considerations, be they broad issues of policy or individual cases.[12]

As a procedural rule, states are required to establish formal processes with stringent procedural safeguards, intended to assess and determine the child's best interests in the taking of decisions which concern him or her, including mechanisms for evaluating the results. States are bound to develop transparent and objective processes for all decisions made by legislators, judges or administrative authorities, especially in areas which directly affect children.

Accordingly, the Committee invites states and all persons who are in a position to assess and determine the child's best interests to pay special attention to certain safeguards and guarantees, such as the right of the child to express his or her own views; establishment of facts; time perception; participation of qualified professionals; adequate legal representation for the child; that any decision concerning a child or children be motivated, justified and explained; the existence of mechanisms allowing a decision concerning a child to be challenged or reviewed if it does not appear to have been taken in accordance with the appropriate procedure for assessing and determining the child's best interests.

This threefold nature (right, principle and procedural rule) is the key for understanding the Committee's perception of the child's best interests. In my opinion, this perception is one of the chief contributions made by the General Comment, and its implications will eventually allow a change to be achieved in the paradigm concerning the child contained in the convention – namely that the child should cease to be regarded by the legal system as an object of protection and be regarded as a subject of law in his or her own right, with all the attendant implications.

---

12. General Comment No. 14 (2013), paragraph 6.c.

The concept of the best interests of the child: what does it add to children's human rights?

Nigel Cantwell
International consultant on child protection policy

The notion of "the best interests of the child" was developed well before the time when children were explicitly granted human rights. Indeed, reference to "best interests" was essentially designed to constitute a standard – albeit a somewhat imprecise one – for decision making on initiatives to be taken in regard to children in the absence of such rights.

Best interests have consequently been invoked in the past in order to justify a wide range of actions. Some of these have been positive, such as Dr Barnardo's move to replace residential placements by foster care, in late 19th century England already.[13] Too many, however, have involved measures that would now be qualified as gross violations of human rights: forced adoptions and forced migration, for example, during several decades in the mid-20th century.[14] At the same time, courts of law in many countries have for many years validly relied on "best interests" considerations notably when determining custody and access conditions in situations of parental divorce.

This article contends, however, that the prominent role now assigned to "best interests of the child" is mistaken and even dangerous in a context where children have human rights. It argues that the implications of applying the concept in the way foreseen by the United Nations Convention on the Rights of the Child (UNCRC) were not thought through and, notwithstanding General Comment No. 14 of the Committee on the Rights of the Child (hereinafter "the Committee"), have not since been addressed in a sufficiently critical manner. As a result, we are now unwarrantedly duty-bound to take systematic account of a basically paternalistic and charitable notion in the implementation of the human rights of children.

---

13. See http://www.barnardos.org.uk/barnardo_s_history.pdf. "The history of Barnardo's".
14. Detailed examples are given in Cantwell N. (2014), *The Best Interests of the Child in Intercountry Adoption*, UNICEF Office of Research, Florence, pp. 7-9.

Best interests in international law

It is first necessary to emphasise the fact that children are the only rights-holders for whom international law foresees consideration of best interests as being essential to realising those rights. The few references to (best) interests in human rights treaties only concern children and relate to very specific issues – and this includes the Convention on the Rights of Persons with Disabilities, adopted in 2006 and thus well after the UNCRC, where the notion is studiously avoided save in regard to children. Likewise, the only private international law conventions that mention best interests are those that deal with children's questions. As for international humanitarian and refugee law, the notion of best interests is quite simply absent from all treaties in these domains.

It is therefore perhaps surprising that so little reflection has been undertaken as to why and how it has been considered unnecessary to ensure that the best interests of rights-holders underpin decision making in regard to the implementation of the human rights of everyone bar children – including particularly vulnerable adults, for example.

Best interests in the UNCRC

The prominent role given to best interests in the UNCRC is, in equal measure, undeniable and thoroughly intriguing. Objectively, it is in fact quite difficult to explain how Article 3.1 of the UNCRC became phrased in such an all-encompassing manner.

To begin with, it is worth noting that the mother of all international texts on children – the 1924 Declaration of the Rights of the Child (Declaration of Geneva) – contains no reference at all to "best interests".

While the committee's General comment No. 14 opines that the subsequent 1959 Declaration on the Rights of the Child "enshrined" the concept,[15] the text of that declaration in fact mentions it only in two very specific and quite limited contexts. First, best interests of the child are to be "the paramount consideration" in the "enactment of laws" enabling the child "to develop physically, mentally, morally, spiritually and socially" (Principle 2). Second, parents and others responsible for the child's upbringing are enjoined to take his or her best interests as "the guiding principle" (Principle 7). Since the 1959 Declaration constituted the basis for Poland's initial proposal for a convention in 1978, this was also the rather restricted perspective (limited to lawmakers and primary caretakers) originally envisaged for the UNCRC.

This proposed draft was, however, rejected as a basis for developing the treaty, and Poland submitted a substantially revised version the following year. It was here that, suddenly and without explanation, the scene was set for best interests to take on a vastly enhanced scope in the UNCRC, henceforth encompassing "all actions concerning children, whether undertaken by their parents, guardians, social or state

---

15. UN Committee on the Rights of the Child, General Comment No. 14 (2013) on the right of the child to have his or her best interests taken as a primary consideration (Article 3.1), paragraph 2.

institutions, and in particular by courts of law and administrative authorities" and retaining the status of "the paramount consideration".[16]

While this formulation was amended somewhat during the drafting – with, notably, reference to parents and guardians being moved elsewhere, legislators reinstated in the list of actors, and "the paramount" downgraded to "a primary" – the desirability and implications of this major shift in mindset were never discussed. Probably the nearest the drafters got to doing so was in reaction to a last-minute and unsuccessful bid by the Venezuelan delegate to provide clearer guidance for interpreting the notion in practice. Hence the all-embracing scope of Article 3.1 with which we are confronted today.

While best interests are, exceptionally, to be "the paramount consideration" in relation to adoption decisions – an issue examined later in this text – this should not mask the fact that they are also similarly the determining criterion in four instances where derogations from specific rights can be envisaged: removing a child from parental care, denying contact with parents, envisaging deprivation of liberty with adults and excluding the presence of parents during judicial proceedings. This special role of best interests as an explicitly foreseen reason for not applying a given right is significant and is taken up again later in this article.

Best interests and the Committee on the Rights of the Child

Once the UNCRC had come into effect in September 1990, the Committee on the Rights of the Child was established and elected, with one of its very first tasks being to draw up the list of issues to be addressed by states parties in their initial reports on implementation. The Committee decided to ask states parties, in the overall context of these reports, to describe their compliance in four spheres that it saw as fundamental, over-arching requirements for implementation: non-discrimination; the right to life, survival and development; the right to be heard; and guarantees that best interests will be a primary consideration in decision making.

The Committee decided to designate these four spheres as being, in its view, "General Principles" of the UNCRC, and thus retaining them as the bedrock of states' subsequent periodic reports. This designation thus stems from the debates of 10 persons whose focus was on developing a questionnaire for states parties, and who unilaterally decided to elevate "best interests of the child" to that special status.

It can be noted that no other treaty body has ever sought to give such prominence to specific provisions of an international instrument. Despite this, best interests have since been, to all intents and purposes, universally and unquestioningly accepted as a general principle, without adherence to which the treaty's implementation would be severely compromised or even impossible.

Given in particular its history of misuse and the legacy thereof, the deliberate flexibility of the concept, its unique pertinence to children's issues in a human rights framework, and the singular importance attached to it by the Committee, it is unfortunate and paradoxical – even though in many ways understandable because of the complexity of

---

16. *Note verbale* dated 5 October 1979, UN Doc E/CN.4/1349.

the issue – that more than 20 years went by before an interpretive General Comment on the implications of applying the "best interests" principle was issued.

However, the Committee's valiant efforts to settle the conceptual and operational quandaries through its General Comment are uncritical, and faithfully reflect the now sacrosanct stance that best interests are a "fundamental value" of the UNCRC, comprising "a right, a principle and a rule of procedure" to be operationalised on all levels and in all circumstances.

That stance needs to be subjected to in-depth scrutiny, more especially to determine precisely what, and when, the notion of best interests actually contributes significantly to safeguarding the human rights of children. Thus, the Committee's list of issues to be taken into account when determining the best interests of an individual child is essentially nothing more than a review of the rights implications of various options; indeed, its proposed procedure to ensure that the child's best interests are a primary consideration in the development of laws and policies is tellingly called a "Child-Rights Impact Assessment". This surely begs the question as to whether best interests really have to be invoked to justify processes designed to evaluate whether or not human rights are being respected and, if that is by chance the case, why for children alone?

The big test: intercountry adoption

One of the most glaring demonstrations of how the application of best interests is still woefully lacking in guidance – and this to the extent that it can anyway be justified – lies in examination of it being "the paramount consideration" for decisions on adoption, and more especially of its intercountry form. While this may constitute an extreme example of the problem, it is instructive since the various facets involved are by no means unique, in some degree at least, to this particular issue.

When intercountry adoption began in earnest, in the early 1950s, it did so in a legal void – procedurally as well as in terms of substantive standards and human rights – and was solely the result of private initiatives. In that context of an absence of norms, it was invariably justified by those private actors as a humanitarian act responding to the best interests of the children concerned.

Despite successive attempts to regulate the practice, the key role of the private sector in the sphere of intercountry adoption has rarely been contested as such, even though it is unusually significant in terms of the provision of a child protection measure and indeed might itself be open to questioning on best interests grounds. Likewise, and of particular note here, the original reliance on best interests as the most important factor justifying intercountry adoption has simply been reaffirmed without question in all subsequent international texts, including those that establish or take inspiration from the human rights framework.

As a result, we have the intriguing situation – although some might argue that the Committee's General Comment has adequately responded to this – where international human rights standards require "the paramount consideration" (that is, the determining factor) in decisions on the adoption of children to be the deliberately vague notion of best interests on which there is no international consensus, rather than demonstrable respect for the rights involved.

Flexibility: a challenge for consensus

The lack of international consensus remains remarkable and preoccupying. While, as noted previously, little has been written on the *raison d'être* of best interests considerations in a human rights context, many commentators have in contrast analysed and defended the need for the notion to be flexible in order, notably, to take account of the different socio-cultural contexts in which it is to be applied (although strangely, this barely finds reflection in the General Comment).[17]

This inevitably presents a special challenge where intercountry adoption and other cross-border issues are concerned. Actors in the socio-cultural context of a country of origin, who in principle bear sole responsibility for determining a child's best interests, may have a very different view of the latter to the one espoused by actors in receiving countries, whose influence on "adoptability" undeniably holds sway in many instances. This was a point made very strongly at a Pan-African Conference on Intercountry Adoption organised by the Africa Child Policy Forum in 2012.[18] Under such circumstances, how is the "paramountcy" of best interests to be assured and proclaimed?

A possibly even more regrettable, and certainly more unfathomable, indication of the absence of consensus lies in the different attitudes taken by receiving countries towards situations in countries of origin where there are clear concerns about the probity of the adoption process, and thus about ability to ensure the primacy of the best interests of the children concerned. Why did only three countries (Ireland, Sweden and the USA) halt adoptions from Vietnam in 2008 because of such concerns? Why, in contrast, did the USA pursue its adoption programme with Guatemala for several years after European countries had withdrawn? Why did the Scandinavian countries and Spain evoke "best interests" concerns to end adoptions from Haiti at the start of this century already, while other European and North American countries were still maintaining that best interests were being systematically respected? The lack of a common baseline – or of the will to impose it – is more than disturbing.

It is also Haiti that provides an additional unfortunate example of how, notwithstanding the UNCRC, "best interests" became a pretext for violating children's human rights. Adoptions from post-earthquake Haiti in 2010 clearly exemplified the fragility of compliance with international standards in disaster situations. Receiving countries spuriously invoked "best interests" to justify circumventing vital established procedures designed to protect the rights of the child, resulting in what was tantamount to the unnecessarily expedited evacuation and forced migration of children for the purpose of adoption abroad, some of whom had not even been officially declared "adoptable", let alone matched and bonded with approved prospective adopters.[19]

---

17. It might be said that this is nonetheless alluded to in paragraph 56 concerning the child's religious and cultural identity.
18. See "Intercountry Adoption: Controversies and Alternatives", Proceedings of the Fifth International Policy Conference on the African Child, ACPF, Addis Ababa, 29-30 May 2012.
19. See Haiti: "'Expediting' intercountry adoptions in the aftermath of a natural disaster... preventing future harm", International Social Service, 2010, Geneva; *World Disasters Report 2012*, International Federation of Red Cross and Red Crescent Societies, 2012, Geneva, pp. 68-70.

There is good cause to believe that the ability to fall back on best interests arguments requiring no real proof and, one dare say, grounded here in emotive paternalism, greatly facilitated these initiatives. They would have been eminently more difficult to justify if the benchmark had rather been fixed simply according to more "traditional" human rights considerations allied with respect for internationally agreed procedures on both adoption and evacuations.

Determining best interests in intercountry adoption: pitfalls and problems

It is certainly true that carrying out a best interests assessment and determination exercise such as that proposed by the Committee in its General Comment would in principle give both process and substance to decision making, and should help to avoid the more arbitrary interpretations – or manipulations[20] – of best interests underpinning reprehensible courses of action. That said, two points have to be raised.

First, these exercises require substantial and qualified human resources that would be hard to envisage in many situations. Second, as noted previously, the assessment essentially involves looking at the extent to which a variety of rights are safeguarded (or not) by any given options; there may therefore be a case for simply ensuring, in the first instance, that core rights relating to identity and family ties would not be violated by whatever action is proposed, and that other rights are then protected. In the end, this is not in fact a question of best interests but of fundamental attachment to the promotion and defence of human rights to be enjoyed by all.

There is a further disturbing element when it comes to elevating best interests to "the paramount consideration" in decisions on adoption. The Committee notes in its General Comment that:

> In the best-interests assessment, one has to consider that the capacities of the child will evolve. Decision-makers should therefore consider measures that can be revised or adjusted accordingly, instead of making definitive and irreversible decisions.[21]

This is perfectly reasonable, but of course it does not rhyme with decisions to be made on adoption which are indeed designed to be "definitive and irreversible". There is no cause at all to take the Committee to task on this issue – it is expressing understandable hesitation as to the longer-term implications of a best interests determination. But it is precisely that hesitation that should spark the question: how, in that light, can best interests possibly be seen as the determining criterion for what is supposed to be a permanent life-changing decision?

When is the notion of best interests counter-productive?

Arguably, then, invoking the notion of best interests is often pointless, sometimes questionable, and even counter-productive in certain situations.

---

20. In its General Comment No. 14, the Committee itself recognises the opportunities that exist for manipulating the concept (paragraph 34).
21. General Comment No. 14 (2013), paragraph 84.

When the concept of the best interests of the child was being incorporated into human rights law, children still had few recognised human rights – and certainly not a codified set of them. "Best interests" had meanwhile become inextricably associated with children's issues, precisely because of that state of affairs. The basic tenets of UNCRC Article 3.1 were established already in 1980, well before the then unforeseen panoply of other rights was debated and finalised. It was not reviewed in the light of that comprehensive range of human rights being accepted, and which by that very fact should have made it often irrelevant – and at worst a potentially negative force in some cases – for implementing the UNCRC with a human rights mindset.

Moreover, the continued and unwarranted plethora of references to best interests, seemingly required by the UNCRC, actually impedes awareness raising about the fact that children have human rights as opposed to "special" rights, and that these rights can and should be defended on the same basis as those of all other human beings, for whom best interests are simply not a human rights issue.

To illustrate these problems, the following are just three of potentially countless recent examples where it could be argued that best interests have been invoked pointlessly, debatably, or erroneously, and detract from the discourse on human rights as such.

First, the International Commission of Jurists (ICJ) has reported a court case in Guatemala where it was "alleged that the State violated through omission the right to food, the rights to life, health, education, and an adequate standard of living and housing, of the children suffering from acute malnutrition in the municipality [in the Department of Zacapa]." While these are clearly and purely issues of human rights (including of the child), the ICJ goes on to note that "the [Court's legal] analysis focused on the principle of the best interests of the child as a person with full legal responsibility". The question therefore arises as to why "best interests" would need to be considered or evoked in such an instance.[22]

Second, the Council of Europe's Commissioner for Human Rights has very rightly highlighted the fact that "protection of children is sometimes evoked as an argument to block the availability of information about LGBTI people to children". He continues:

> There is no evidence that dissemination of information advocating a positive attitude towards LGBTI people would adversely affect children. Rather it is in the best interests of children to be informed about sexuality and gender diversity.[23]

This comment raises questions, however: how have those best interests been determined and by whom, and why would it be necessary anyway to use that notion as the basis for a judgment on a human rights issue? Surely the same argument could be made equally well on the basis of non-discrimination and UNCRC Article 13 (right to access to information) bearing in mind the restrictions stipulated in that provision. Advancing best interests might therefore be contested as an attempt, in part at least, to nullify limitations to the exercise of that human right as foreseen by the treaty.

22. Cases No. 19003-2011-00638-Of.1a; No. 19003-2011-00639-Of.2a; No. 19003-2011-00637-Of.3a; No. 19003-2011-00641-Of.1 (2013).
23. Council of Europe Commissioner for Human Rights, Human Rights Comment, "LGBTI children have the right to safety and equality", 2 October 2014.

Third, the Child Rights International Network carries a report[24] that: "Hungary's Equal Treatment Authority found a school guilty of unlawful discrimination for rejecting the application of a [13-year-old] boy because he was raised by same-sex parents." The school had "claimed that their decision was in the best interests of the boy to prevent potential bullying". In this case, best interests had been invoked in order, implicitly, to try to justify non-compliance with the right to education and to protection from non-discrimination. The mere recognition of best interests of the child as a General Principle of the UNCRC surely tends to provoke or promote such responses; while the latter may be successfully combatted after the event in many cases, the overall misleading message sent can be that best interests are on an equal yet different footing to children's human rights – or even some kind of "super right".

What are the positive contributions of best interests?

Human rights – including those of children – can invariably be observed and defended quite simply as human rights. There is no a priori assumption that the promotion and protection of human rights in general, individually or collectively, are at risk of being undertaken in ways or for reasons that might be detrimental to the rights-holders concerned or to their interests.

It is therefore difficult to understand why a contrary assumption might be deemed to apply validly to children alone, and this to such an extent that it needs to be explicitly stated – and constantly and actively upheld – that their interests are to be a primary or, in some circumstances, even a paramount consideration.

Yet decision making on the basis of the best interests of the child can undoubtedly contribute to compliance with children's human rights in specific circumstances. Somewhat paradoxically and albeit in a new context, we need to be returning to a vision of the function of best interests as it was in the era before the UNCRC in order to ensure such a positive contribution.

In essence, that vision is of filling a gap – or gaps – in rights provision rather than underpinning the assurance of all human rights of children. By implication this includes situations where rights considerations alone do not provide sufficient guidance or grounds for decision making. Nowadays a clear human rights framework in which best interests are to be interpreted and operationalised sets a number of boundaries that cannot be lightly crossed: together with a recognised determination process, this should in principle provide some form of guarantee against the kind of unacceptable outcomes that were all too common in the past.

From that standpoint and under those conditions, there are many situations where assessing best interests can be useful, not to say vital. Most have already been acknowledged – including in the Committee's General Comment – and they comprise decisions involving in particular: choosing between two or more potential solutions that are, a priori, all consistent with the human rights of the child concerned; real or apparent conflict between two or more rights; issues not covered by existing rights; and situations where the interests of other parties might otherwise jeopardise or unduly influence outcomes for the child.

---

24. CRINmail No. 1397, 1 October 2014.

Furthermore, best interests can be validly invoked to justify derogation from a given right when the possibility of doing so is already explicitly established in the UNCRC, and notably: removal from parental care/family environment (Articles 9.1 and 20.1); denial of contact with parents (Article 9.3); non-separation from adults in detention (Article 37.*c*) and prohibition of parental presence during judicial proceedings (Article 40.2.*b*.iii).

This in itself constitutes a sufficiently challenging list. Our attention should be more especially focused on ensuring appropriate responses in these situations. It is neither justified nor desirable that we feel compelled to consider best interests as expressing "one of the fundamental values of the [UNCRC]"[25] that need to be actively assessed and reflected in relation to all rights and situations, regardless of whether or not reference to them meaningfully advances the cause of the human rights of children in those instances.

By way of conclusion

But we cannot turn back the clock. The best interests of the child are now an integral part of human rights law as it applies to children, and we are therefore obliged to deal with this reality. It is undoubtedly helpful that, through its long-awaited General Comment, the Committee has now underlined the need to avoid subjective and arbitrary pronouncements on children's best interests and thus to set in place an accepted and systematic process to assess and determine those interests.

In so doing, however, the Committee clearly embraced its task by taking the notion and apparent importance of best interests at face value rather than adopting a more critical stance. It therefore lost the opportunity to develop a more nuanced interpretation which could have set best interests determination in a wider human rights context, indicating the limitations on its pertinence therein.

As this article has sought to demonstrate, there are indeed good grounds for broaching "best interests" in a somewhat more circumspect manner than has been the case to date. Those grounds include the genesis and history of the notion itself, the way in which it became incorporated into the UNCRC, the problem of locating it in a human rights framework, its ongoing manipulative usage, and the importance often given to "interests"-based arguments to the detriment of rights-based thrusts. The point is not to deny that the proper determination of best interests has a role in the implementation of the UNCRC, but to ensure that it is called upon to play that role only when necessary, appropriate and feasible as a tool for advancing the human rights of children.

---

25. General comment No. 14 (2013), paragraph 1.

Interpreting and applying the best interests of the child: the main challenges

Olga Khazova
Associate Professor at the Institute of State and Law, Russian Academy of Sciences, Moscow; member of the UN Committee on the Rights of the Child

This article discusses the main challenges in interpreting and applying the concept of the best interests of the child. I will first present some general considerations, then specific issues related to family cases and finally some procedural issues in the application of this concept in practice. The discussion will be based not only on what was highlighted during the European Conference on the Best Interests of the Child, but also on what we have learned from academic writings, the jurisprudence of the European Court of Human Rights and, of course, from General Comment No. 14 (2013) of the UN Committee on the Rights of the Child on the right of the child to have his or her best interests taken as a primary consideration (Article 3.1). It will hopefully help to define the legal guidelines that would support professionals and policy makers in their everyday work on protection of children's rights.

The concept of the best interests of the child has been the subject of more academic analysis than any other concept included in the United Nations Convention on the Rights of the Child (UNCRC). It is one of the most important – if not the most important – concepts in the child right's context. However, it is one of the most difficult concepts to apply in practice. Many distinguished scholars have tried to define it or create a list of factors that are central when defining what is or is not in the best interests of a certain child. But so far, no one has developed with a comprehensive definition that would be workable without exceptions for different purposes and in every situation. Mostly due to this, many academics and practitioners have strongly criticised this concept.

Indeed, the concept is to a certain extent vague and sometimes leads to misunderstanding and confusion. On the other hand, it is due to its vagueness that the concept of the best interests of the child is applicable to very different situations where a child's interests are at stake. Flexibility comes at a price of vagueness.

One of the common critical arguments is that the concept of the best interests of the child reflects a paternalistic approach, and in that sense it can be considered as a remnant from the past. However, it is important to differentiate between the principle of the best interests of the child and the welfare principle. The welfare principle values welfare and does not concentrate on rights. Although the welfare principle and the best interests of the child principle have a lot in common, they differ from each other. It is the term "welfare" that has a paternalistic, protective connotation. The best interests of the child, on the opposite, is interpreted as a right, and also as a legal principle, and a rule of procedure. In this context I would emphasise its dimension as a substantive right.

The concept of the best interests of the child lies at the core of the UNCRC and underpins the rights set out in its articles. Because of the crucial importance of this concept and of numerous requests for its clarification, the Committee on the Rights of the Child adopted General Comment No. 14 in 2013. We are often asked why it took the Committee 20 years to develop a General Comment clarifying the implementation of the concept. The answer was given at the conference, "because it was extraordinarily difficult". Although it is too early now to evaluate this General Comment and more time is needed, there is no doubt the General Comment will contribute to a better understanding of the principle of the best interests of the child and advance its more correct and effective application.

In practice, there are many difficulties related to the application of the principle of the best interests of the child. I will emphasise the two that seem to be the most important.

The first one is the difficulty of assessment of what is in the best interests of the child. The concept of the best interests of the child is child specific. Therefore, as stated in General Comment No. 14, its content "must be determined on a case-by-case basis".[26] What is in the best interests of one child may not be in the best interests of another child in a similar situation.

The second difficulty is connected with the goal to strike a balance between different interests. What is in the best interests of one child often competes with the interests of other persons, for instance parents, and more importantly, with what is in the best interests of another child or other children – siblings, for instance.

There are many factors that need to be taken into account when assessing what is in the best interests of a specific individual child or group of children. General Comment No. 14 indicates seven elements that should help in such assessments. In some countries, legislators have developed very detailed lists of factors to be considered by a judge or other specialist when making a decision regarding a child or children.

Application of the best interests of the child standard creates especially difficult problems in family-related cases. If we abstract ourselves from the specific situation of a particular child and try to identify at a very general level what is the most important for a child – what is the first consideration for a child with regard to different family-related situations? It seems the following can be stated.

---

26. UN Committee on the Rights of the Child, General Comment No. 14 (2013) on the right of the child to have his or her best interests taken as a primary consideration (Article 3.1), paragraph 32.

First, as far as custody disputes in divorce or parental separation cases are concerned, it is necessary to ensure that the child can maintain close contact with both parents (except in situations when this may be harmful for a child). A detailed list of elements or factors could help us decide how this can be practically done. However, the main goal, to repeat, is to ensure that the child is not deprived of the luxury of having both parents.

Second, poverty, bad housing and a poor environment are clearly not in the best interests of any child. But does it mean that the children should be removed from their parents if the parents are not in a position to cope with the economic and social difficulties? The jurisprudence of the European Court of Human Rights gives an answer to this question and sets up guidelines. In the cases of *Wallová and Walla v. Czech Republic* (2006)[27] and *Saviny v. Ukraine* (2008)[28] national authorities, instead of helping the parents cope with their social and economic difficulties, placed their children in care. According to the Court, the families should have received support instead. This is a message to those who are involved in making decisions on removal of children from their families. In this regard, migrant families often require additional attention in order to avoid discriminatory situations.

Third, the concept of best interests of the child in the context of what is sometimes called "alternative families" is increasingly becoming an evolving issue in Europe. Although same-sex couples with children and different conflicts over children that arise in these families are still "new territory", we may find some guidance in case law. A good example is a United Kingdom Court of Appeal case *A. v. B. & C.*, where the court suggested a solution for a dispute between a lesbian couple and a biological father. In deciding what was in the child's best interests, the court found it important to identify "the source of the child's nurture, stability and security". In some cases it may be a two-parent family and in other cases it may be a three-parent and two-home regime. "Disruptions to that security and stability", even if arising indirectly, will be "relevant as potentially harmful to the child".[29] In this regard, particular consideration should be given to the part that each adult could play in the child's life. This is also an example that demonstrates how the concept of the child's best interests changes over time.

Fourth, determining what is in the child's best interests and trying to strike a balance create special problems in cases where children were born as a result of assisted reproduction, were adopted, were abandoned by their mothers who gave birth anonymously or in other similar situations. These issues are very different from each other, most of them are very new and some of them are extremely controversial. Therefore, it is necessary to approach them individually and, accordingly, try to find individual solutions to each of the scenarios. At the same time, whatever the regulation may be, the child shall have the right to get access to the information about his or her origins.

The fifth and the last main question to address here is procedural issues related to the application of the best interests of the child standard. In this context, a central

---

27. *Wallová and Walla v. the Czech Republic*, no. 23848/04, 26 October 2006.
28. *Saviny v. Ukraine*, no. 39948/06, 18 December 2008.
29. *A v B and C* [2012] EWCA Civ 285, paragraph 45.

theme is child participation, which is a transversal issue that has a prominent role in a best-interests assessment. In accordance with Article 12 of the UNCRC, a child has the right "to have a say" in all matters affecting him or her, and the child should be able to exercise this right. Our task is to create an effective mechanism to ensure the child's participation.

In addition to participation, another important theme related to procedural issues is that in all cases on child custody, removal of children from home, and in similar situations, it is necessary to combine the goal of stability and finality of a decision on a child's placement and the possibility of revision of this final decision. When making a decision, it is important to examine its potential consequences and try to predict what might be better for the child in the future. To make such a decision, it is necessary to work within a group of professionals: a judge, a psychologist, a pedagogue, perhaps a medical professional, or others, depending on each situation. The multidisciplinary approach is a key to success.

There is a desperate need for training for all groups of professionals at all levels in order to help them properly interpret and apply the concept of the best interests of the child. To make such training more efficient, it would perhaps be beneficial to elaborate a collection of best approaches, good practices, good decisions, solutions and ideas that could be applicable to family cases. This collection would equally demonstrate the specificity of the best interests of the child in regard to different types of family cases.

Best interests of the child and the right to be heard

Gerison Lansdown
International child-rights consultant

Article 3 of the United Nations Convention on the Rights of the Child (UNCRC), embodying the concept of the best interests of the child, is a unique provision in a human rights treaty, establishing a principle to guide decisions and actions affecting the lives of children both individually and collectively. It was introduced in recognition of the fact that children, in common with adults, are subjects of human rights, but unlike adults, they do not have presumptive autonomy and the right to independent decision making in respect of their own lives. On the contrary, in childhood, that presumption is reversed with the entitlement to exercise rights on their own behalf only acquired gradually throughout childhood, depending on their own evolving capacities and the legislative environment in which they are living. Full autonomy is not usually afforded until 18 years of age.

The best interests principle was therefore introduced to provide boundaries and focus through which those adults who are empowered to make decisions on behalf of children as individuals, as well as at the wider policy level, should be guided. It applies in the first instance to parents, but also to all others with authority over children's lives or whose actions impact on children – courts, social workers, police, doctors, nurses, teachers, law and policy makers and others. It is, therefore, a principle of fundamental importance, intended to provide a positive and constructive obligation to orientate decisions to ensure the overall well-being of children.

However, wrongly understood or applied, it may serve to undermine or threaten the realisation of the rights of the child. It can be, and often is, used as a "trump card" to justify any action that adults with power over children choose to make. History is littered with examples of adult policies and actions, promoted at the time as being in the best interests of children, but subsequently discredited – for example, the evacuation of children during the Second World War, the refusal to allow mothers contact with children in hospital, corporal punishment, the institutionalisation of children or the application of shock treatments to "cure" children with disabilities. In other words, adults are far from omniscient in respect of their capacities to determine children's best interests.

In order to address these concerns and promote positive application of the principle, the Committee on the Rights of the Child has provided guidance on its interpretation. The Committee argues that the concept of best interests is a substantive right, an interpretative principle and a rule of procedure.[30] Its application must always be guided by the UNCRC itself. First, all actions affecting children must be directed towards the realisation of their rights. No action can be justified as being in a child's best interests if it serves to violate those rights. Female genital mutilation, for example, cannot be defended on grounds that it is in the best interests of the girl to be cut in order to be accepted within her culture, or promote her marriageability. It violates her fundamental dignity, right to protection from all forms of violence and abuse, to freedom from cruel or inhuman treatment, and to optimum development and the best possible health.

Second, it is important to adopt a holistic approach to the realisation of children's rights. For example, measures to guarantee a child the right to the best possible health cannot be effective through the provision of health services alone. Consideration must also be afforded to the child's right to family life, to education, to play, to an adequate standard of living, to appropriate nutrition and access to clean water, as well as to privacy. Additionally, and of profound significance, the determination of best interests must take account of the views of the child, in accordance with age and maturity, and allow for increasing autonomy in the determination of his or her own best interests in accordance with evolving capacities.

These approaches to the determination of the child's best interests are encapsulated in Figure 1.

Figure 1: Evolving capacities, views of the child and substantive UNCRC rights as components of a best interests of the child determination.

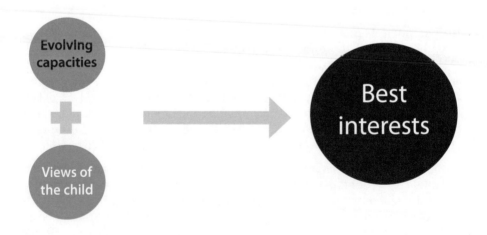

---

30. UN Committee on the Rights of the Child, General Comment No.14 (2013) on the right of the child to have his or her best interests taken as a primary consideration (Article 3.1), paragraph 6.

Article 5 of the UNCRC, which introduces the concept of the evolving capacities of the child, provides the transitional linkage between the initial dependency of a newborn child and the full autonomy afforded to an adult. Children necessarily rely on adult direction and guidance during the period of their childhood as their capacities evolve. However, Article 5 imposes clear boundaries on the exercise of that guidance. It states that any guidance by parents or other caregivers must be appropriate, consistent with the evolving capacities of the child and directed to the exercise by the child of his or her human rights. In other words, parents are not free simply to decide for themselves what is in their child's best interests. They must ensure that their actions and decisions are consistent with the child's rights and that they gradually allow for a transfer of decision making from the adult to the child as the child acquires the capacity to take responsibility for him or herself.[31]

Article 12 complements Article 5 by asserting that in all matters affecting children, they have a right to express their views and have them taken seriously. The determination of best interests, accordingly, must be rights-oriented, influenced by the views of the child, and take account of the capacities of the child to make decisions for him or herself. The importance of recognising children's participation rights, together with respect for their evolving capacities as the means through which to enhance or understand their best interests, has application for the UNCRC in its entirety.

The UNCRC explicitly recognises the child as a subject of rights and an active agent in the exercise of these rights, through not only Article 12, but also the rights to freedom of expression, thought, conscience and religion, association, to privacy and to information, all affirm children's agency. Respect for these rights is consistent with promoting their best interests. The Committee on the Rights of the Child has emphasised that Article 12 is not only a fundamental right, but also a principle that must be applied in the realisation of all other rights. A growing body of evidence testifies to the benefits that accrue to the child through the experience of being listened to, valued and respected, including greater self-confidence, acquisition of skills, and improved mental health and well-being.[32] Furthermore, as space is created for children to express their views and have opportunities to inform decisions affecting them as individuals as well as at the broader societal level, it is clear that they contribute significantly to the process of enabling adults in positions of power to arrive at decisions and outcomes directed to their best interests.

Many rights in the UNCRC, the so-called provision rights, are directed towards the overall development of the child – for example, rights to education, play, health care, social security, family life or an adequate standard of living. Clearly the fulfilment of these rights will contribute towards the optimum development and well-being of children, and thereby the promotion of their best interests. However, they will all be more effectively realised if the child's right to be heard informs their implementation. For example, children not only benefit more from their education if they are recognised and respected as active participants in their own learning, but they can also provide invaluable expertise to the overall learning environment through school

---

31. General Comment No.14 (2013), paragraph 44.
32. See, for example, European Commission (2015), *Evaluation of legislation, policy and practice on children's participation in the European Union*, Publications Office of the European Union, Luxembourg.

councils, contributions to school policies, and feedback on teaching methods and the curriculum and wider education policy.[33]

Children's involvement in health care is increasingly recognised as integral to ensuring the best health outcomes. The Child-to-Child methodology, for example, was developed in the 1980s based on the principle that children could work together to bring about positive change. It subsequently rolled out a model of active engagement of children in promoting health education messages and guidance in thousands of communities around the world. It was rooted in recognition of children's capacities to take responsibility for aspects of their own and local communities' health needs, and thereby promoting their own and others' best interests.[34]

Furthermore, decisions by courts on family placement, adoption or care plans are all enhanced if meaningful opportunities are created for the child's views and experiences to be sought and taken into account. The recent EU evaluation of child participation across member states, for example, found that there is "a clear link between children successfully exercising their right to be heard, and tangible improvements to their status or personal circumstances".[35] In other words, it is not possible to pursue the optimum development of the child, and his or her best interests, if the child's perspectives are disregarded.

The UNCRC clearly acknowledges that children are entitled to additional protections in view of their greater vulnerability and "still evolving capacities". The rights to protection from violence, economic and sexual exploitation, armed conflict; to minimum ages of marriage or entry into full time work, or to alternative care when necessary, affirm that adults have very clear responsibilities to guarantee that children are not exposed to harm and risk that will be detrimental to their best interests.

However, in the field of protection, as with all other rights, the interests of children will be best served through a commitment to ensuring that their voices are heard. Protection is commonly viewed as being provided by adults with the child as the passive recipient. In fact, protection is far more effective when children themselves are empowered to speak out. There is now widespread evidence that the failure to listen to children has played a major contributory role in allowing widespread sexual abuse and exploitation of children to go uncovered or challenged for years – in the church, in institutions, in communities, in the family.[36] Where children are consistently silenced, disbelieved and lacking any safe avenue for complaint, the outcome is impunity for abusers. Only by listening to children is it possible to ensure their best interests through effective protection. And children often have a far clearer understanding of the risks they face, the nature of the violence they are exposed to and the possible strategies that are needed to bring it to an end.

---

33. See, for example, UNICEF, "Impact of the Rights Respecting Schools Award on schools".
34. Child to Child, "Our history".
35. European Commission (2015), op. cit.
36. See, for example, reports of inquiries into sexual and physical abuse in the UK and Republic of Ireland: *The Pindown Experience and the Protection of Children: The Report of the Staffordshire Child Care Enquiry*, Levy A. and Kahan B., Staffordshire County Council, 1991; *The Leicestershire Inquiry 1992*, Kirkwood A. (Leicestershire County Council 1993); *Lost In Care*, the Tribunal of Inquiry into abuse of children in care in Clwyd and Gwynedd, Sir Ronald Waterhouse, DH/Welsh Office 2000; *The Report of the Commission of Inquiry into Child Abuse*, Republic of Ireland, 2009.

The obligation to ensure that the best interests of the child is a primary consideration in all actions affecting them is far from straightforward. It can and has been used to justify far too many laws, policies, and individual decisions which have been detrimental and damaging to children. However, the risk of its misapplication arises when it is adopted as a stand-alone principle, or as a trump to override all other perspectives. It is not and should never be viewed in isolation. It must be applied through the lens of the UNCRC as a whole, and determined with appropriate respect for children's own views and respect for their right to take increasing responsibilities for decisions in accordance with their evolving capacities. If, and only if these circumstances prevail, it can serve as a vital organising and mediating principle to help direct actions affecting children, contribute to the determination of difficult and complex decisions affecting children's lives, and guide the development of policies, services and resources impacting on children.

Alpha ursae minoris – The North Star and the child's best interests among competing interests

Jacques Fierens

Professor at the University of Namur and the University of Liège, honorary member of the Brussels Bar Association

Alpha ursae minoris, the brightest star in the *Ursa Minor* or Little Bear constellation, is better known by the name of the "North Star". It is 2 100 light years away from Earth. Like all stars, far from being immutable or static, it has a life of its own, its own temperature variations and a specific mass. If it were to die, we on Earth would take more than two millennia to notice. It can be seen only from the Northern Hemisphere. It appears very small in the glowing sky of a summer's night, even though it is brighter than billions of others. Did you know that the axis of the Earth oscillates, and that as a result, through the centuries and millennia, the North Star has not always been the same?

Gazing at it, as at any star, inspires thoughts and dreams and opens the mind to the mysteries of the existence of the Earth and mankind in the cosmos. It is often difficult to see because of cloud cover or intense stray light sources nearby. It is totally invisible in sunlight. The fame of *Alpha ursae minoris* comes primarily from its ability to guide travellers, especially sailors. It permitted the discoveries which we attribute to the explorers, but in fact they could not work without this speck of light, so small and so essential.

The principle of respect for the child's best interests is to the law what the North Star is to the night sky. It is difficult to grasp, attracting many criticisms from those who only believe what they can touch, smell and hold in their hands and from those who think it necessary to know everything about the volume, density and composition of the child's interests for this principle to guide them. However, it can fulfil its function in countless situations, from countless different positions, in response to countless different questions on which direction to take.

The child's best interests are part of what the theorists call notions with variable content. The closer you come to the very foundations of legal systems, the more you encounter these notions whose meanings are always indefinite: equality, proportionality, equity, public order, good morals, or quite simply "justice". The principle of the child's best interests has no foreordained substance. It is undefinable until one is faced with a specific situation. That is its function: making us first of all remain silent, cut stray light sources and look at who the child is. I am wary of grids of indicators and pseudo-mathematical formulae which will spit out the formula of the child's best interests. You could just as well replace judges with computers.

The North Star indicates a direction and allows for measurement, which is also possible with instruments as simple as a compass or a sextant. The concept of a child's best interests fills the same role. It is not a philosophical viewpoint to be debated, but a legal concept, hence a vehicle for action. That is how General Comment No. 14 of the Committee on the Rights of the Child would have us understand it. The comment does not speak of content but of balancing interests, of fundamental interpretative principles and of procedural rules. This text is not in itself a star, but indicates a direction, the conditions for correct observation of the constellations, and the exact direction in which the decision maker should point the telescope, according to place and time. General Comment No. 14 is the astronomer's guide.

The child's best interests should be a "primary consideration". There are almost as many divergent interests as there are stars in the sky, but the child holds a central place; his or her brightness is a more important indication than all others. Sometimes nothing else is seen, as if the night had nothing in it but the North Star. This is obviously an illusion. The observer thus imagines that the child's best interests are opposed, in principle, to the interests of others, especially his or her parents. That is the risk arising from individualism, which would have us believe that a child can conceive himself, in every sense of the word. On the contrary, the child's best interests are part of a constellation forming part of a system belonging to a universe. This concept contributes to the delineation of harmonious shapes, as lovely as a small bear nestling against the Great Bear constellation. It has relations with the other stars who do not oppose it. The United Nations Convention on the Rights of the Child (UNCRC), moreover, enshrines not only individual rights of the child, it considers the child in relation to others, especially in his or her family.

However, it is true that often, other closer, yet far less powerful, lights normally prevent the child's interests from being taken as a primary consideration. The interfering glare of adult selfishness, financial interests, immigration police and purported imperatives of security or social defence often make *Alpha ursae minoris* totally invisible. Then children are separated from their families, torn between their parents, ill-treated by institutions, confined behind barbed wire or put in prison. Even the European Court of Human Rights sometimes lets itself be blinded by stray lights, especially where it seems to conform to a kind of principle of reality by accepting that migrant children and their families should receive lesser protection than the families of nationals. The Strasbourg Court does not hesitate to interpret the European Convention on Human Rights in conjunction with the UNCRC, but one sometimes has the impression that it gives up viewing the firmament, that it turns its eye from the telescope to look at the ground. One never sees the stars while looking down.

The child's best interests are an interpretative principle. To interpret means endeavouring to understand what is said. Yes indeed, the principle of a child's best interests speaks, converses with statute and judge, because the child speaks, whatever his or her age, however *in-fans* ("unable to speak") or deemed incapable of self-expression. Even stars are listened to. Huge antennas have been built to hear what they say, especially when the wavelength which they emit is imperceptible to the eye but may yet be perceptible to the ear. Listening to a child and heeding his or her interests cannot be done off the cuff; it involves a learning process, resources, knowledge and a lot of ambient silence. Knowing how to interpret the stars and planets is one of the world's oldest wisdoms, but informed interpreters are rare. Everyone considers him or herself capable of it, however it is not enough to stroll absentmindedly.

The child's best interests indicate a procedure to follow, the obligation for any decision maker to take bearings, to determine exactly the decreasing or increasing angle between the North Star and the horizon. What captain would venture to steer his boat without regularly checking that it follows the chosen course? Letting oneself be guided by a star other than that of the child's best interests would be most imprudent also. All other stars, those of all other interests, revolve around this North Star, and following them would make us go round in circles indefinitely, while waiting to be shipwrecked.

To tell the truth, I find that the expression of Article 3 of the Convention on the Rights of the Child is not the most apt. The term "interests" has a self-interested, egocentric, perhaps even slightly capitalistic connotation. I would have preferred "the respect due to the child". Perhaps the vocabulary is dependent on that time when the concept came into being, more remote than is thought, but when all is said and done very recent, above all compared to the life of a star. It is also the vocabulary of burgeoning hard core liberalism in which the overriding interest is financial.

It is not the UNCRC that invented the concept, or the 1960s. Its trace is already found in the preparatory papers for Napoleon's Civil Code. One would need to research the question for other legal traditions. In the northern part of the planet, when society as a whole recognised the specificity of childhood, the law followed suit, a few years behind as always. With the exception of the inspirational Rousseau, a pioneer in the matter, this period is probably placed in the second half of the 19th century and the early decades of the 20th century. Consider the literature of the time: Charles Dickens' *Oliver Twist* in 1837, Lewis Carroll's *Alice's Adventures in Wonderland* in 1865, the Countess of Ségur's *Un bon petit diable* in 1865, Carlo Collodi's *The Adventures of Pinocchio* in 1883, Frank Wedekind and *Spring Awakening* in 1891, Rudyard Kipling and *The Jungle Book* in 1894.

I confess I have a very special interest in the story of Mowgli, which is a remarkable exploration of a child's relationship with his father, mother and family, accompanied by a portrayal of the predators threatening him, through a striking meditation on observance of the law as a condition of community living and through a reminder of the place of Law in children's upbringing. Once society as a whole acknowledges children's singularity, their fundamental rights can be proclaimed. This is what happened for the first time in 1924 in the first Declaration of the Rights of the Child, thanks in particular to Eglantyne Jebb. What happened afterwards is well known: the influence of Janusz Korczak, the 1959 UN Declaration of the Rights of the Child and the UNCRC, the most-ratified treaty on fundamental rights, nevertheless constantly violated by the rich and powerful just as all their legal undertakings in favour of a more humane world.

There is no cause to deny that the North Star of the child's best interests is a more effective and better understood, if not better respected, guide in the Northern Hemisphere than in the rest of the world. That does not mean the southern countries violate the rights of the child more than the others because they are lacking in civilisation, more uncouth or incapable of respect for the weak. It is nevertheless important to realise that human rights in general, and the rights of the child in particular, were generated by a culture and a history that is not shared by many families in the world. The countenance of the child which emerges from the UNCRC is that of a European or North American child, not an African, Chinese or Arab child. The intention is not to lapse into general relativism. The rights of the child must be respected, protected and realised all over the world. They are exportable with no cultural imperialism intended. The convention must retain its universal purpose. However, one should be particularly alert to the difficulties of reception stemming from the peculiarities of place and time which surrounded the birth of these rights. It is a form of necessary respect for all who, often justifiably, take a different view of children than "Westerners".

I know very well that there are GPS tracking devices, far more widely used today than stars to get one's bearings. Therein lies the danger: the technology of adults claiming to supplant for good a very distant speck of light. The child's best interests nevertheless have advantages over GPS. It can never break down. It is there even when no longer powered. It will always be an essential benchmark when all alternative methods for determining what is right have proved inadequate. Good old North Star. It seems very small, like a child lost in a huge crowd, but how enormous it must be if one comes close enough!

Children's best interests: a discussion of commonly encountered tensions

A report by the Children's Rights Knowledge Centre (KeKi)
Eveline van Hooijdonk
Children's Rights Knowledge Centre

In light of the European Conference on the Best Interests of the Child, to celebrate the 25th anniversary of the United Nations Convention on the Rights of the Child (UNCRC), the Children's Rights Knowledge Centre (in Dutch Kenniscentrum Kinderrechten, abbreviated as KeKi)[37] conducted a study to uncover common points of tension in the translation of the principle of the best interests of the child from theory to practice.[38] The investigation was a study commissioned by the Division for Youth of the Flemish Government.

Through an inventory and content analysis of existing international best-interests practices and policy initiatives since 2004,[39] KeKi found four common points of tension: workability of the best-interests principle in practical situations, conflicts of interest, an instrumental view of participation and protecting children's best interests on a policy level. We discovered these points of tension through screening of online databases (www.kekidatabank.be and www.kinderrechtencoalitie.be) by using the keywords: *"Belang van het kind"* (the best interests of the child in Dutch), "Child best interests", "children's best interests" and "best interests of the child". As the scope of the analysis was limited, we believe that the four points of tension are just "the tip of the iceberg". In this text, the points of tension that were found and possible solutions to address them are discussed. The solutions recommend further development and promotion of a best-interests framework that is applicable to children's daily realities.

---

37. For more information, see www.keki.be/en.
38. Op de Beeck H., Herbots K., Lembrechts S., Willems N. and Vlieghe K. (2014), *Children's best interests between theory and practice, a discussion of commonly encountered tensions and possible solutions based on international best interests practices and policy strategies since 2004*, KEKI.
39. See the appendix of the report for examples and the complete overview of the screening.

First of all, as the content analysis suggests, the formulation of a substantive inter-pretation of the best interests of the child principle that is applicable to a broad variety of individual situations is difficult. The principle appears to be inevitably indeterminate, flexible, dynamic, developmentally dependent and context specific. This has consequences for the workability of the principle in practical situations. In the report, we tried to answer the following question: What kind of framework can be developed to avoid the concept becoming hollow and meaningless, or being used in a tokenistic way?

The study found that it is possible to develop a factual interpretation of the best interests principle. This can be done with the help of a solid scientific methodology.[40] On the other hand, it might be necessary to simply accept the lack of a generally applicable interpretation of the principle, since every context requires a different reading of it. The report suggests a clear and general decision-making procedure or structure for best-interests assessments. Such a procedure or structure will decrease the influence of underlying assumptions by rationalising the decision-making pro-cess. A clear decision-making structure can serve as a general procedural guideline in all best-interests assessments.

One can also focus on procedural elements to come to an adequate assessment, which we see as a learning trajectory. Adults, together with children, learn about what is best for the child. To develop such a learning experience, inspiration can be found in mediation mechanisms and practices that are specifically directed towards learning about each other's perspective.

The findings from the content analysis suggest that the background, knowledge and communicative skills of the individual who performs the best interests assessment may be more important than the tool that is used for the assessment. Best interests determinations are not merely a matter of applying a certain instrument or filling out a checklist. Several initiatives in our content analysis focus on training and education. The professional should have the necessary competences to perform the assessment as adequately and holistically as possible. Especially in cases in which important decisions are taken by individuals whose main experiences or skills are not neces-sarily child specific – such as return decisions taken by immigration judges – training may bring added value. Different educational programmes and practical training packages also exist. These packages can serve as an inspiration for policy makers or practitioners who wish to set up a child-specific programme. Such a programme can contain, for instance, elements of child psychology, development perspective and a child-rights perspective. Finally, an *ex-post* or feedback system allows the professional to learn about the consequences of his or her decision. Monitoring and feedback lead to more varied knowledge and experience. The professional will then take more appropriate decisions in the future.

The second theme the study highlighted was that assessing children's best interests does not take place in a vacuum. Different contexts play a role, and consequently,

---

40. Kalverboer M. and Zijstra E. (2006), *Het belang van het kind in het Nederlands recht: Voorwaarden voor ontwikkeling vanuit pedagogisch perspectief*, Uitgeverij SWP. For an in-depth article on the development of a factual interpretation of the best-interests principle, see Kalverboer's text in this publication, Chapter 2.2.

children's interests may at times conflict with interests of other parties involved. In referring to Article 3.1 of the UNCRC, Smeyers argues that "[c]learly, this requirement cannot be enforced without regard to the interest of any relevant adult".[41] As well, Eekelaar criticises the fact that, due to the strong focus on children's best interests, no proper consideration is paid to the interests of other involved parties.[42] We found initiatives that describe how the concept of the best interests of the child can in practice be "hijacked" or misused to defend interests of other parties. Below, we give some means of avoiding the misuse of the child best interests.

The study found five clear examples of conflicting interests: child custody in divorce cases, decisions regarding placement in or returning from care, children whose parents are imprisoned, parental authority in child health decisions and decisions in immigration cases. The first example illustrates that even though it is generally assumed that parents will first and foremost defend their child's interests, the interests of parents and children can conflict. Due to their own wishes or the situation, both parties – and caretakers or other family members – can have differing opinions on what is best for the child.

Also, the child's best interests can be misused to defend other parties' wishes. Therefore we suggest clearly separating children's interests from their parents' or other parties' interests. The last example, decisions in immigration cases, shows the conflict in interests between society and the child. Society decides that the parents should leave the country of immigration, and the interests of the child are often understood as an extension of the parents' interests. Leaving the country is not always in the best interests of the child. To avoid this conflict, a transparent distinct definition of other parties' interests should be created and adequate methodologies to safeguard all interests should be developed.

The third finding of the study is related to the importance of children's own views. When determining the best interests of a child, it is essential to know what the child himself or herself considers to be his or her best interests. In the inventoried projects, participation is mainly used in an instrumental way, as a means to acquire understanding of what the child feels, thinks and believes is in his or her best interests. Hearing the child's voice and taking his or her perspective into consideration are essential in coming to good best interests decisions. In light of meaningful participation, different authors and practitioners are cautious to avoid tokenism, negative participation and "over-querying" of children. In our analysis, we found suggestions to sustain participation and broaden it in individual decisions as well as in collective decisions.

In order to let children participate, it is important to adequately inform them. The information should be in their own language and adapted to their level of understanding. Even though children can participate in many different ways, an important cause of tension is that in practice the capability, age and maturity of the child remain too strongly a point of reference in deciding if and how a child can participate in

---

41. Smeyers P. (2010), "Child rearing in the 'risk' society: on the discourse of rights and the 'best interests of a child'", *Educational Theory*, Vol. 60, No. 3, Wiley-Blackwell, p. 277.
42. Eekelaar J. (2005), "Deciding for Children", *Australian Journal of Professional and Applied Ethics*, Vol. 7, No. 2, pp. 66-82.

determining his or her best interests. Capability and maturity cannot be defined in general terms, a case-by-case assessment is always necessary. An individual maturity test can support a professional in determining the best mode of participation and the weight allocated to the child's opinion. Inspirational good practices for developing a maturity test can be found in the study.

Next, a decision has to be made between direct and indirect participation. Direct participation means that the child participates in the decision-making process him or herself as an equal, next to the other involved stakeholders. We speak of indirect participation when the child is represented by a close family member or a trained professional who expresses the child's wishes and needs based on close communications with the child. If the child has not yet acquired the maturity to be directly involved, indirect participation through representation is a possibility. We found two examples of such practices.[43]

Listening to children's voices is not only important in individual decisions. In collective decisions, such as policy decisions, children's voices are crucial as well. In this case, an important challenge arising from the content analysis is the assurance of an equal representation. Socially vulnerable children and youth have a higher risk of being excluded from participatory trajectories. A non-exhaustive list of strategies to address this challenge, such as co-operation with target-group-specific organisations, the development of adjusted methodologies and representative sampling methods, was suggested based on existing participation and social research practices.

Finally, the study found that in different countries or regions, initiatives have been developed to protect children's interests at the macro level. Examples of this kind of initiative include shaping a child-friendly legislative framework through the application of child (rights) impact assessments, child standards and other instruments that are directed at the maximisation of positive and the minimisation of negative consequences of new legislation or (policy) decisions for children and youth. Child-rights impact assessments are brought forward in General Comment No. 14 by the Committee on the Rights of the Child as crucial instruments to shape an optimal frame of reference for individual best-interests assessments. They procedurally relate to best interests assessments, as both kinds of assessment include an *ex-ante* reflective process regarding the impact of important decisions on children's lives.

Therefore, the study argues that child-rights impact assessments and best interests assessments can be an inspiration for original solutions to existing shortcomings. In conducting a successful best interests assessment, it is essential to centralise knowledge and expertise regarding these assessments and make them accessible through online modalities and through the support of a network of informed focal points. It is also important to facilitate control and appeal of policy decisions that directly and indirectly affect children, as well as to take into account the social context of the child. Especially in decisions that only indirectly affect children, balancing the different interests involved may be a precarious exercise. It also has to be kept in mind that it is not the eventual outcome, but the underlying reflections that are capital in

---

43. National Society for the Prevention of Cruelty to Children (2012), *Returning home from care: what's best for children*; Bilson A. and White S. (2005), "Representing children's views and best interests in court: an international comparison", *Child Abuse Review*, Wiley-Blackwell, Vol. 14, No. 4.

best-interests assessments. The procedural character of determining children's best interests should be underlined.

In conclusion, the study conducted by KeKi showed that practitioners worldwide are not discouraged by theoretical difficulties and the vagueness related to the best interests principle. The study found creative ways to effectively use this concept in different professional situations. It is important to invest in child-specific training programmes for professionals as well as in monitoring, feedback and *ex-post* evaluation. Children's interests should be clearly distinguished from other parties' interests, and children's meaningful participation in decisions affecting them should be a priority both for individual and collective decisions. Inspiration for best interests assessments can be found in child-rights impact assessments. The dialogue between theoretical inspiration and practical creativity creates pathways for real progress and proficiency.

Chapter 2

Assessing, determining and monitoring best interests

Determining marginalised children's best interests through meaningful participation

Lessons learned from the pedagogy of Janusz Korczak

Urszula Markowska-Manista
PhD, lecturer and researcher, Chair of Basic Education and UNESCO/ Janusz Korczak Chair, Interdisciplinary Studies in Child Development and Well-being, Maria Grzegorzewska University

It would be a mistake to think that to understand means to avoid difficulties.[44]

This text[45] discusses Janusz Korczak's theory of practical involvement of children in their rights, in particular the emancipation interest, and integrates his principles in the analysis of research on children's everyday lives. First I will refer to the research on everyday life environments of marginalised, discriminated and excluded children, children living in poverty and on the social margin, frequently categorised as children "out of place".[46] This is a category created by adults which refers to, among other things, socially, culturally and politically excluded groups of children who live

---

44. Korczak J. (1993), *Selected works*, volume 7: *How to love a child. A child in a family,* Warsaw, Oficyna Wydawnicza Latona.
45. I would like to thank Prof. Manfred Liebel and Aleksandra Borzecka for their comments and advice in the preparation of this text.
46. More on the subject, among others: Penn H., Unequal Childhoods. Young children's lives in poor countries, London: Routledge, 2005, pp. 1-44; See also Ennew J., Hastadewi Y., Plateau D. P., Seen, Heard – and Forgotten? Participation of children and young people in Southeast, East Asia and Pacific in events and forums leading to and following up on the United Nations General Assembly Special Session for Children. Children, Youth and Environments 17(1), 2007. It must be added that the term children "out of place" operates also in a critical approach. This subject is addressed by: Liebel M. and Budde R., Other Children, Other Youth: Against Eurocentrism in Childhood and Youth Research; Bourdillon M., Thinking about street children and orphans in Africa: beyond survival, in a book under preparation: Children out-of-Place and Human Rights: in Memory of Judith Ennew, eds. by Invernizzi A., Liebel M., Milne B. and Budde R., Springer, 2016.

in an era of a global crisis (economic, humanitarian), and who are "unheard" in the majority discourse due to their place of residence (the peripheries, distanced from the centres, in countries defined as "developing" or in the grips of conflicts and wars). These unheard children are of lower social status and inherit a stigma of "the inferior", and also frequently experience inherited discrimination and marginalisation. They do not always have the possibility to participate in the decisions of the majority society, and their access to human rights is limited and problematic. Their access to rights or lack thereof, reflects their class and position in social structures. The above factors and their inhibited access to secondary and higher level education place them in the category of a "lost generation" and at a crossroads between tradition (customary law) and modernity (domestic and international law). These children, due to the marginal environments they belong to, are also placed in the category of "invisible" children.[47] The question that arises at this point is, can we, adults in the contemporary world, speak about the balance between the concept of a child's best interests (Article 3) and the right to life, survival and development (Article 6) of the United Nations Convention on the Rights of the Child (UNCRC)?

I then search for an answer to the question: how do we involve marginalised children in the determination of their own best interests?[48] I shall outline examples of activities with children for children's rights realised by the Polish-Jewish doctor, pedagogue and social activist Janusz Korczak. It must be stressed that these activities took place in different conditions and several decades ago. However, the attitude to children and his ideas and methods of co-operation with and for children seem universal, and can be adapted to the contemporary world and the contemporary challenges and problems, particularly in regards to the current situation of children and their parents escaping threats to their health and lives in territories torn with wars and conflicts. These examples will be illustrations of activities and attempts to design solutions based on the contemporary reading of Korczak's thought, on humble and intent listening to children's voices. In Janusz Korczak's words,

> In upbringing everything is an experiment, an attempt. I try in a gentle and strict way, I try to encourage and prevent, I try to accelerate and delay, I try to diminish and exaggerate. We do not intend to renounce the program of trials for the sake of a despotic dogma. An attempt ought to be cautious, prudent, not to expose to danger – and our system of upbringing is such an attempt.[49]

---

47. Books S. (ed.) (2003), Invisible children in the society and its schools, Routledge; Books S., (ed.) (2006), Invisible children in the society and its schools, Third Edition, Routledge; Naylor A., Prescott P. (2004), "Invisible children? The need for support groups for siblings of disabled children", British Journal of Special Education, 31.4, pp. 199-206; UNICEF (2006), The State of the World's Children 2006 – Excluded and Invisible, New York.
48. The subject of the multidimensionality of children's interests is addressed in Liebel M.(2015), Kinderinteressen. Zwischen Paternalismus und Partizipation, Beltz-Juventa, Weinheim & Basel.
49. Weekly magazine Bursy: [no title, I], [in:] Korczak J., Dzieła (2008), Selected works, vol. 1, Warsaw, p. 12.

Marginalised children

The world we live in, the contemporary world, has opened new doors for children but also created new problems.[50] On the one hand, we have a variety of tools to protect children against violations of their rights (the UNCRC and its additional protocols,[51] the African Charter on the Rights and Welfare of the Child[52] and many others important declarations). On the other hand, we observe a reality which is not always helpful and child friendly despite the letter of the law and aid activities realised by international and non-governmental organisations. Researchers indicate that economic and social inequalities of children's life environments push them to the margin. These inequalities make it impossible for them to "be a child"[53] and create disparities in their chances.[54] Inequalities limit children's potential for development and education as well as participation in the design of structures and economy of the states where they live.

A number of academic and popular science articles published in recent years describe the urgent problems experienced by millions of children in the labyrinths of the adult world. These problems of children who are left alone, the victims of a dysfunctional family, social and political life are of a global character. They concern the whole world as young refugees, migrants, displaced persons and children without documents, make up a permanent element of societies in the "Global South" as well as countries considered to be failed. For instance, in my article "Children and youth – refugees and 'non-citizens' as a socially inconvenient category. The excluded generation in Dadaab",[55] I draw attention to the fact that the life stories of refugee children and youth who have experienced conflicts in the country of their origin, recruitment into the army or rebel groups, the stigma of massacres, acts of violence, poverty, hunger, diseases, psychological and physical exhaustion following their escape, are placed in the category of the "socially inconvenient". These life stories also reveal that we are helpless in the face of violations of written and unwritten children's rights.

---

50. More on the subject in UNICEF (2014), 25 years of the Convention on the Rights of the Child – Is the world a better place for children? A recent report by the UNICEF Office of Research indicates that nearly 76.5 million children live in poverty in the 41 richest countries of the world. The children's poverty index has risen not only in developing countries but also in developed countries. Governments' ability to reduce poverty among children has been weakened. See UNICEF Office of Research (2014), Children of the Recession: The impact of the economic crisis on child well-being in rich countries, Innocenti Report Card 12, UNICEF Office of Research, Florence.
51. Optional Protocol to the Convention on the Rights of the Child on the involvement of children in armed conflict, Optional Protocol to the Convention on the Rights of the Child on the sale of children, child prostitution and child pornography; Optional Protocol to the Convention on the Rights of the Child on a communications procedure.
52. OAU Doc. CAB/LEG/24.9/49 (1990), entered into force on November 29, 1999.
53. With reference to a right to childhood and a right to be a child, thus a right to play, grow and develop in conditions which are friendly and safe – this right was promoted by J. Korczak.
54. Research on the influence of poverty and inequalities on children on various continents and in various environments is presented in the report: Woodhead M., Dornan P. and Murray H. (2013), What Inequality Means for Children. Evidence from Young Lives, Young Lives.
55. Markowska-Manista U. (2013), "Dzieci i młodzież - uchodźcy i 'nieobywatele' jako kategoria społecznie niewygodna. Wykluczone pokolenie w Dadaab" ("Children and youth – refugees and 'non-citizens' as a socially inconvenient category. The excluded generation in Dadaab"), in A. M. Kłonkowska, M.Szulc (eds), Społecznie wykluczeni. Niewygodni, nienormatywni, nieprzystosowani, nieadekwatni, Gdańsk, pp. 111-128.

It is enough to look at the map of the world which is pulsating with migration and refugees and consider the reasons why Article 22 of the UNCRC, which states that refugee children shall receive appropriate protection and humanitarian assistance in the enjoyment of applicable rights set forth in the UNCRC and in other international human rights or humanitarian instruments, is in praxis defunct in many countries. And yet, almost all countries in the world have signed the UNCRC.

Certain mechanisms for children's protection operating in the countries of the Global North and the Global South are becoming dysfunctional in an increasingly diversified, fluid, heterogeneous and contradictory reality. The situation is also affected by the transformations related to the collapse of the political concept of multiculturalism in western countries of the European Union; the "journeys of despair";[56] the tragedies in the Mediterranean Sea and on the border between Greece and Macedonia and in the Eurotunnel; the dramatic situation in the overcrowded refugee camps in Greece and Italy or the chaos in societies on the African, Asian and European continents. It seems that the legal standards which were to facilitate children's protection and their rights overwhelm us and leave us helpless. As a result, "the wrongs done by the powers which elude control on the negatively globalized planet are countless and ubiquitous – but above all: diffused and blurry".[57]

In the contemporary world, marginalisation, discrimination, exploitation and exclusion are a tangled web of factors that make adults, and children along with them, slip to the social margin. An individual and collective, common and academic perspective on the events in a global and local space, both the public, social and the personal one, fills the contemporary man with fear. For the majority of human beings, the world's margins are the everyday "life-worlds"[58] of children, where there is no possibility to fully or partly participate in an excessively complex and confusing reality. These life-worlds are not only geographically distant from the perspective of the "Western" world (the Global North), but also distant with regard to access to goods and rights. They are life-worlds of children whose voices remain unheard in the global media discourse, in international debates and even in the dimension of mainstream aid provision at the local level.

We are frequently faced with images and statistics showing children who suffer and who are pushed and categorised into the roles of refugees, migrants, orphans, child soldiers, abused children, working children, street children, child soldiers prepared to kill and fight in wars. The list of these categories seems endless. Statistics often undermine our ability to take sensible actions aimed at solving children's problems that should be approached not merely from a material, but a psychological and educational perspective. We need effective action, not people hiding behind statistics.

56. See Liberti S. (2011), *A sud di Lampedusa* („South of Lampedusa"), Rome.
57. Bauman Z. (2008), *Płynny lęk*, translated by J.Margański, Wydawnictwo Literackie, Kraków.
58. The category of an everyday "life-world" (*Lebenswelt*) is an interdisciplinary one as researchers indicate it is difficult to present a clear-cut and precise definition of an everyday life-world. It comprises everyday experiences, everyday activities of an individual, his or her dreams and impressions in the sphere of *sacrum* and *profanum*. An everyday life-world from an anthropological perspective constitutes a specific kind of obviousness, which is a social and cultural product, an effect of collective work done in a particular group which is conditioned both by internal and external factors.

Indigenous peoples' children – as it is among them that I conducted my research[59] and it is to them that I would like to refer – belong today to one of the most discriminated groups in the world and to extremely marginalised communities. They are a category of children who are "out of place". They are "invisible", living in poverty and in the margins of society. They are victims of a process of transformation shaped by their place in the social structure and past life experiences, as well as entanglement in relations with and dependence on other social groups.[60]

Social marginalisation and the fact of remaining outside the mainstream of social life as well as limited access to education are tantamount to "holding positions which are socially peripheral".[61] This means "lesser rights with often wider duties, lesser possibilities to take decisions and choose, worse social and economic situation, lower educational, professional and health care possibilities".[62] Marginality explains the reality as individuals and marginal groups, including children, experience voluntary isolation and/or isolation imposed by outer conditions. Moreover, they do not participate on an equal level with the non-marginalised part of the society in the most important spheres of life. They tend to play the role of passive observers or subservient performers of certain tasks. They hardly ever become initiators and/or full participants.[63] The "otherness" and the inferior position imposed by the dominant groups stratify, exclude, introduce divisions and push disadvantaged groups to the margin, or beyond the margin of rights and social privileges.[64]

As a process which threatens a child's proper development, and consequently the development of a particular minority group, marginalisation constitutes a serious obstacle in the functioning[65] of children from indigenous groups, children belonging to ethnic minorities or refugee children. While analysing in the course of my field research[66] the rich anthropological literature on hunter-gatherer peoples in Central Africa, I noticed that relatively little attention is paid to the issue of childhood or children's problems and their place in a tribal community facing the civilisational

---

59. Author's research and research projects completed between 2002 and 2012 among the Ba'Aka Pygmies in the Central African Republic.
60. What I have in mind here are colonial and postcolonial experiences as well as contemporary global dependencies.
61. Kowalak T. (2001), "Social marginalisation", in B. Rysz-Kowalczyk (ed.), Leksykon polityki społecznej (Social politics lexicon), ASPRA-JR, Warsaw.
62. Based on Psyk-Piotrowska E., Demarginalizacja wsi drogą: urbanizacji, skansenizacji, samodzielnego rozwoju (Demarginalisation of rural areas as a way to: urbanisation, open-air musealisation, independent development).
63. The fragment in question comes from Markowska-Manista U. (2012), "Obszary dyskryminacji i marginalizacji Pigmejów w Afryce Środkowej" (The areas of discrimination and marginalisation of Pygmies in Central Africa), in Jarecka-Stępień K., Kościółek J. (ed.), Problemy współczesnej Afryki. Szanse i wyzwania na przyszłość (The problems of contemporary Africa. Chances and challenges for the future), Księgarnia Akademicka, Kraków, pp. 83-97.
64. More on the subject in Jarosz M. (2008), "Obszary wykluczenia w Polsce" (Areas of exclusion in Poland) in Wykluczeni, wymiar społeczny, materialny i etniczny (The excluded, the social, material and ethnic dimension), Instytut Studiów Politycznych PAN, Warsaw, pp. 10-11.
65. I use the word functioning, which may be perceived by the readers as technocratic, with reference to the multidimensional existence of the child in the world and his or her varied activities.
66. A study within the research projects, "A child's right to education as a condition and a chance of its social emancipation. A diagnosis of the state of ORA method education among the Bantu, Ba'Aka and Mbororo in a culturally and ethnically heterogeneous region: Monasao and Belemboke in Central African Republic", "Everyday life of Ba'Aka children in Central African Republic" 2002-2012.

transformations taking place in the world. Traditional hunter-gatherers' children often constitute about 40% of their population. Thus, nearly a half of the population remains invisible.[67] This problem has recently been included in wider anthropological, ethnographic, psychological and politological research on development transformations,[68] conflicts, health, migration and mobility, cross-cultural and African studies.[69] Yet, it must be stressed that children who are rejected and ignored in social practices aimed at individual and social development; marginalised children, and among them street children and working children, are not "(…) 'objects of concern', but people. They are vulnerable but not incapable. They need respect, not pity."[70]

One of the researchers who drew attention to "invisible" children in her research and study results was Judith Ennew, an activist and researcher in children's rights who began working in 1979. She directed her research and practical activities at children's "unwritten rights". She claimed that children, in particular discriminated and socially excluded children, have a right to an honest description, research and counting.[71] She expressed her opposition to random statistics and the lack of high-quality, systematic research and information on children's lives and their everyday experiences. She drew attention to the dominant "victimising" approach, not only in regard to childhood studies but also the practice of professionals working with children.[72]

An answer to the common victimising approach could be research which gives "prime importance to child participation".[73] Research done in "socially sensitive" places and spaces enables one to turn to the perspective of children who do not have a voice, who are voiceless, who are "seen but not heard", as Ennew writes.[74] It could provide a deeper insight and perspective into children's everyday lives and a broader perspective in the analysis of their problems. In other words, these emancipation studies would include and involve children and give them a voice. They would also take into

---

67. After Hewlett B.S. and Lamb M.E. (2005), *Hunter-gatherer Childhoods: Evolutionary, Developmental & Cultural Perspectives*, Transaction Publishers, New Brunswick, New Jersey.
68. More at www.developmenttransformations.com.
69. See B. Hewlett's research at Washington State University Vancouver concerning the anthropology of childhood in a cultural perspective, A. Wrzesińska's research on children in Cameroon presented in the book: *MWANA znaczy dziecko* (MWANA means a child), DIALOG, Wyd. Akademickie, Warsaw, 2005.
70. Ennew J. (1994), *Street and Working Children: A guide to planning*, Save the Children, London, p. 35, also cited [in:] Panter-Brick C. (2002), "Street Children, Human Rights, and Public Health: A Critique and Future Directions", *Annual Review of Anthropology*, Vol. 31, p. 156.
71. Boyden J. and Ennew J. (1997), *Children in focus: a manual for participatory research with children*, Rädda Barnen; Beazley H., Bessell S., Ennew J. and Waterson R. (2009), *The right to be properly researched: Research with children in a messy, real world*, pp. 365-378.
72. Ennew J. and Swart-Kruger J. (2003), "Introduction: Homes, Places and Spaces in the Construction of Street Children and Street Youth", *Children, Youth and Environments*, 13(1).
73. Panter-Brick C. (2002), "Street Children, Human Rights, and Public Health: A Critique and Future Directions".
74. See Ennew J., Hastadewi Y. and Plateau D.P. (2007), "Seen, Heard – and Forgotten? Participation of children and young people in Southeast, East Asia and Pacific in events and forums leading to and following up on the United Nations General Assembly Special Session for Children", *Children, Youth and Environments* 17(1); Liebel M. and Cussiánovich A. discussed the question during the International Symposium in Memory of Judith Ennew – "Children Out-of-Place and Human Rights", Free University Berlin, October 27-28, 2014.

account varied situations and conditions of a child's functioning[75] not only from the position of an adult observer. Thus, we need research with children rather than about children.[76] In this type of research, as Manfred Liebel points out:

> it should be taken into account that not all children are in the same situation or have the same problems. The examples of research done by working children demonstrate that children must have the chance to form their own identities and formulate their own questions and aims for research, starting from their own experiences and priorities.[77]

Janusz Korczak's lessons

On 5 December 2012, during a ceremony which summarised the commemoration of the International Congress on Children's Rights organised by the Ombudsman for Children in Warsaw, the "Warsaw Declaration" was adopted. This symbolic document refers to the ideas of a great pedagogue, doctor and children's friend – Janusz Korczak, nicknamed "The Old Doctor". His writings remind us of children's inalienable dignity, their empowerment and the value of life of each and every human being. The declaration states as follows:

The basis of Korczak's philosophy is a wise love for the child, a recognition of the child's status as a subject, a child's dignity, freedom, and responsibility, a respect for the child's right to respect, to bonds of partnership in family, society and state. The child is a citizen whose voice must be heard in personal and family matters, as well as social and national ones.

> The declaration urges adults – parents, educators and caregivers, teachers, politicians, clerics and all people responsible for the shape of social life – to undertake actions for ensuring that each child leads a happy life in a world without violence, discrimination, wilful neglect and other ill-treatment. It is a call for the realisation of Janusz Korczak's legacy in contemporary reality, of children's life among adults.

Everyone who speaks about Korczak today faces a difficult task. On the one hand, they have to face the image of a hero, a heroic legend, a secular "saint" who devoted his life to orphaned children; on the other hand, a statuesque icon of children's rights and the creator of an original educational system. Much has been written about Korczak. Dozens of his biographies, memoirs, innumerable popular science texts and academic articles have been published. And yet, taking into consideration the

---

75. More on the subject, among others: Thomson P. (2008), "Children and young people: Voices in visual research", in Thomson P. (ed.), Doing Visual Research with Children and Young People, Taylor & Francis London, pp. 3-19; Kellett M. (2005), Children as active researchers: a new research paradigm for the 21st century?, ESRC, UK; Powell M. A., Graham A., Taylor N.J., Newell S. and Fitzgerald R. (2011), Building Capacity for Ethical Research with Children and Young People: An International Research Project to Examine the Ethical Issues and Challenges in Undertaking Research with and for Children in Different Majority and Minority World Contexts (Research Report for the Childwatch International Research Network), Dunedin, University of Otago Centre for Research on Children and Families & Lismore: Centre for Children and Young People; Save the Children (2004), So You Want to Involve Children in Research? A toolkit supporting children's meaningful and ethical participation in research relating to violence against children, Stockholm.
76. The problem is subjected to a multifaceted analysis in Liebel M., "Child-led Research: Experiences with Working Children in the Majority World", CREAN Conference "Children's Rights Research: From Theory to Practice", Madrid, September 24-25, 2013 [unpublished version].
77. Liebel M., "Child-led Research: Experiences with Working Children in the Majority World".

versatility and timeless validity of his considerations on children, still not everything has been said about him and his "pedagogy of everything". Korczak's pedagogy, present in many of his writings, takes into account the transformations taking place in education about and for children's rights in the world. Despite the passage of time, Korczak's pedagogy is still relevant and has spread worldwide. The continued interest in Korczak is a testimony to this fact. His legacy and thought live among researchers, pedagogues and those working with children and supporting them, for instance, in the European Union countries, Japan, Canada, Kazakhstan, Ukraine, Argentina, Brazil, Israel, the Democratic Republic of Congo, Benin or Ivory Coast.[78]

However, there arises a problem of reading Korczak today, that is reading Korczak in contemporary times in the reality of a multicultural, globalised world in which one faces disturbances connected with racism, exploitation, violation of rights, degradation of the natural environment, the unequal relations of power, gender, class and religion. It is a world troubled by new dimensions of migration and refugeeism, both of adults and children, by a double and multidimensional identity, poverty and exclusion, haunted by wars and conflicts which continue and escalate in various parts of the globe. Thus, there is still relevance in Korczak's thesis that, when relating to a child, one must not violate a mutual right to freedom and a life in dignity, to functioning in everyday reality. Korczak practised this ideal. He did not close off the world to children. On the contrary, he tried to open the world to them. As a paediatrician and educator he entered into real contact with a child. He worked, accompanied, was present, talked, taught, played, joked, discussed. He was authentic by filling children's everyday reality with a practice of co-participation in development and by supporting this development. He indicated that an educator should always adapt his or her approach and direction of action to particular conditions and particular children in given situations and contexts.

Korczak included his pedagogical ideas primarily in the tetralogy *How to love a child* (1920), *A child's right to respect* (1929), *The rules of life* (1930) and *Playful pedagogy* (1939), as well as a number of other works. In these texts he called for a recognition of the fact that from the moment of birth a child is a full person, worthy of respect, and remains so at each stage of existence. According to Korczak, a child has a right to be himself or herself. The Old Doctor treated children as equal citizens.

> Korczak's children's rights are inextricably connected with development. Development and well-being, development and moral standards. A child has a right to sin, to err, to ignorance. A child is good, the greatest good and it does good. … A child is a person, a child is a human being. Not a being predisposed to be human, but human here and now – as Korczak would say.[79]

These ideas found their reflection and development in his modern, anti-authoritarian system of education. The system was based on various forms of activity, participation and children's self-governance in a children's society in which children govern themselves and punish each other in peer tribunals for disobeying the law. The system

---

78. These are activities initiated by individuals belonging to Janusz Korczak Associations and the International Janusz Korczak Association (IKA) in various countries of the world or those who co-operate with them.
79. Smolińska-Theiss B. (2010), "Korczakowska idea praw dziecka" (Korczak's idea on the rights of the child), *Pedagogika Społeczna*, No. 3-4.

respected children's needs and aspirations and at the same time urged children to work on themselves and encouraged them to be active and independent. Through a subjective treatment of his pupils, giving them access to organs and instruments to govern, Korczak prepared them for adult life: responsibility, self-governance, deciding about themselves and influencing what happens in a society. It is worth raising the question: What activities helped Korczak realise the innovative concept of a self-governing community?

One of the examples of Korczak's innovative activities and at the same time "one of the most extraordinary experiments in the history of the press"[80] is the newspaper *The Little Review*[81] written by children, for children and adults and referring to their problems and ways of perceiving the world- non-fiction.[82] Children had a right to speak and their texts were to help in their daily lives. Some of them, in fact, had evident results of support, understanding, being noticed, making others aware and solving problems.

Korczak used to say that *The Little Review* was different from all other publications in the world. The newspaper was published in Poland for 13 years (from 1926 to 1939), the circulation was as high as 50 000 copies, and it enabled children's participation in the media discourse as well as allowed for a discussion and for their voices to be heard. The *Little Review* was created by children. Initially Korczak, as well as young editors, edited the texts.

> Today it can be said that *The Little Review* functioned as a social platform avant la lettre. What amazes in the publication is its interactive and two-way character. A part of the newspaper's formula was its constant reference to the readers' and correspondents' opinions. Particularly in the first period, when Korczak was the chief editor, children could count on the Old Editor to answer their letters, to advise, comment or criticise.[83]

The idea behind the review was to organise a children's society based on justice, brotherhood and equal rights and duties.[84] This several-page supplement to the daily newspaper *Our Review* still remains a press phenomenon on a global scale. Despite the passage of time it shows the innovative character of Korczak's pedagogy, who, being ahead of his times (which were not friendly for children), wrote: "A child has a right to serious treatment of its problems, to their just consideration."[85]

The second example of Korczak's innovative activities are peer tribunals which, based on a constitution developed in the orphanage, dealt with all possible cases

80. Gliński M. (2014), "*Mały Przegląd* zdygitalizowany" (*The Little Review* digitalised).

81. The Little Review – a children's newspaper founded by Janusz Korczak in 1926 and published in Warsaw. It was a weekly supplement to a Jewish daily newspaper Our Review.

82. It is a category of texts referring to the real world, the reality surrounding us and in which children perceived and sensed the actual problems of the adult world.

83. Gliński M. (2014), *Mały Przegląd - gazeta inna niż wszystkie* (*The Little Review* – a newspaper unlike any other).

84. Falska M. (1983), Zarys organizacji pracy wychowawczej w "Naszym Domu" (An outline of educational work organisation in "Our House"), in *Myśl pedagogiczna Janusza Korczaka. Nowe źródła*, Wybór M. Falkowska, (Korczak's idea on the rights of the child. New Sources. A selection by M. Falkowska) Nasza Księgarnia, Warsaw, p. 302.

85. Korczak J. (1928), in M. Rogowska-Falska, *Zakład Wychowawczy "Nasz Dom". Szkic Informacyjny ze słowem wstępnym Janusza Korczaka* (The Educational Institution "Our House". "An informative outline with a preface by Janusz Korczak"), Warsaw, p. 33.

of breaking the law.[86] These tribunals judged not only children, but also adults. The role of judges in peer tribunals was played by children themselves (including five pupils constituting a judicial team), as, in Korczak's words, "a child is a good assessor of its life". There was a special code stating that:

> If a person has done something wrong, it is best to forgive him or her, if the wrong was done unintentionally, he or she will be more cautious in the future … If a person has done something wrong having been encouraged to do so, he or she will not listen to others anymore. If a person does something wrong it is better to forgive him or her, wait for an improvement. But the tribunal must defend the quiet so that the pugnacious and intrusive ones would not hurt them, the tribunal must defend the weak so that the strong ones would not trouble them, the tribunal must defend the conscientious and hard-working so that the careless and lazy ones would not bother them, the tribunal must see to it that there is order, as disorder hurts the good, honest and conscientious people most. The tribunal is not justice, yet it should strive for justice, the tribunal is not the truth, yet it desires the truth.[87]

As many as 99 of the 100 paragraphs of this code had an absolving nature or referred to dismissing a case in question.

Peer tribunals played a significant role in educating and activating children. Korczak draws attention to the fact that this form of children's activity changed the position of a pupil in the nurture process. He uses his own example as an illustration of an educator whose behaviour is also subject to trial.

> In the course of six months I handed myself in for the tribunal's judgment five times. Once for giving a boy a thick ear, once for throwing a boy out of the bedroom, once for putting one in a naughty corner, once for offending the judge […] these few cases were a cornerstone of my education as an honest, constitutional educator who does not harm children not because he likes or loves them, but because there is an institution which defends them against lawlessness, arbitrariness and despotism.[88]

The third example of children's mobilisation, understood as a recognition of their right to speak and influence decisions (co-governing) concerning community life, is the self-government council and children's parliament. As the highest organ of "a children's republic", the children's parliament decided on, among other things, the more important holidays and events in the life of the orphanage. Among its tasks was to approve and reject the laws proposed by the self-government council which consisted of 10 pupils[89] and one guardian. It was an elected institution, meeting in session once a week, which contributed to the development of self-governing. "In the best interests of the child", the council undertook actions which were part of an educational prophylaxis.

By developing the self-government council and children's parliament, Korczak found a solution to a number of problems strictly connected with activating and

---

86. Hammarberg T. (2013), "Korczak helps us understand the rights of the child", in Smolińska-Theiss B. (ed.), *The Year of Janusz Korczak 2012. There are no children, there are people*, Warsaw, p. 48.
87. Rogowska-Falska M. (1928), *Zakład Wychowawczy „Nasz Dom" Szkic Informacyjny ze słowem wstępnym Janusza Korczaka* Warsaw, pp. 33-34, http://www.dbc.wroc.pl/Content/15712/RP%201590.pdf.
88. Korczak J. (1957), *Wybór pism pedagogicznych* (A selection of pedagogical texts), T. I, Warsaw, p. 259.
89. The members of the council could be individuals with a high status. Additionally, they were subject to a general plebiscite.

socialising pupils. Involvement in the work of these two government institutions had an educational impact. It enabled children and youth to participate in an active organisation. The initiatives enriched children's everyday life, taught them social skills as individuals and in groups and offered a way for children and adults to co-operate in a meaningful way.

Korczak not only propagated the best interests of the child, but through practical activities in a dialogue with children – with reference to particular situations – tried to define what these best interests are for them. By following this principle, Korczak enriched his pedagogical concepts taking into account various forms of educational impact. Among them the following deserve attention: duty shifts, children's care of other children, a plebiscite for kindness and dislike, signing in a book of thanks and apologies, awarding with commemorative postcards, establishing notaries, a loan office, sport clubs, a circle of useful entertainment, a scientific circle and the pupils' sports club "Fire", which had its own budget.

Korczak emphasised responsible children's rights. He stressed that a child should conform to a children's community and organisation of laws created by it. The Old Doctor urged adults to follow the rules established by them for children as well as to respect a child's right to speak and make decisions. He accentuated the principle and practice of partnership in the nurturing process. To nurture is to support a child's development, individuality and curiosity about the world. The idea was not to repress and force a pupil to perceive the reality the way adults see it. A child has a right to his or her individuality and uniqueness. An adult is to put effort into understanding a child, into discovering by accompanying him or her in everyday tasks.

It must be stressed that Korczak was aware of the fact that people may not accept his philosophy, that they may not understand the message and reject its content. After all, he wrote: "I call for magna carta libertatis, for children's rights".[90] He was also aware of the fact that the world of adults would not become 100 per cent friendly to children.

Conclusions

Today, having at our disposal a wide range of international and domestic instruments in the form of documents and legal solutions, we, adults, are searching for a way to support children in gaining access to their rights, in guaranteeing their subjective and active participation in everyday life and ensuring the best interests of the child. However, we can see that these instruments and strategies which are to protect children from violations of their rights are not always effective. This becomes apparent, for instance, in children's large-scale participation in armed conflicts as child soldiers, in forced child labour, in employing children in banned jobs or employing those who are too young to work. The multitude of ways in which children are harmed and abused cannot be reflected in numbers.

---

90. Korczak J. (1998), *Jak kochać dziecko* (How to love a child), Wyd. Jacek Santorski, Warszawa.

Korczak experienced the worst conditions of children's lives, the dimensions of their marginalisation, exclusion and poverty.[91] Thus, in his writing and educational praxis he undertook an innovative attempt to determine the best interests of the child and indicated that children are active participants of social life, that they work for their rights. Korczak was a pioneer in the field of children's rights and supported a multifaceted approach to their functioning in the world. He placed children and adults as guardians of children's rights, at the same time attempted to draw the world's attention to the mutual dependence of adults and children: "We educate you but you also educate us."[92] Thus, the question posed at the beginning returns: How do we involve a child in the determination of his or her own best interests?

Lessons learned from an educational point of view based on the heritage of Janusz Korczak can be helpful in searching for an answer. This can be particularly true when looking at the category of children "out of place" and "invisible" children and their position in the society which is unequal in many dimensions of their everyday lives. Activities which facilitate and support children's involvement in the determination of their own best interests cannot be the result of a coincidence but an effect of thorough knowledge about the children and their environment. This must not be an imposed activity, based on the child's dependence on adults discussed by Korczak – also valid today – but participatory activity in which adults acknowledge that a child is a fully valued person from the moment of birth, and at each stage of his or her existence.

What can also be useful is becoming aware of the fact that we, adults, will be able to speak about the balance between the principle of the child's best interests (Article 3 of the UNCRC) and the right to life, survival and development (Article 6 of the UNCRC) only when we accept that we can change the world and that the change begins with improving the lives of adults and children. It is a chain of mutual connections.

---

91. In 1901 he published, among others, articles *Nędza Warszawy* (The poverty of Warsaw) and *Dzieci Ulicy* (Street children).
92. Korczak J., "Trzeba to rozumieć" (It must be understood), in Janusz Korczak w getcie. Nowe źródła (Janusz Korczak in the ghetto. New Sources). An introduction and scientific editing by Lewin A. Text integration Ziółek M. Footnotes Ciesielska M., Falkowska M., Matysiak M., Warsaw, 1992, p. 184.

How to assess and determine the best interests of the child from a perspective of child development and child-rearing

Margrite Kalverboer
Professor of Child, Pedagogy and Migration Law, Faculty of Behavioural and Social Sciences, Department Orthopedagogy, University of Groningen

In 2011, the joint non-governmental organisations for children's rights in the Netherlands submitted the Best Interests of the Child methods (BIC methods) to the United Nations Committee on the Rights of the Child to make a contribution to the discussion of the contents of Article 3 of the United Nations Convention on the Rights of the Child (UNCRC). On 29 May 2013, the Committee issued its General Comment No. 14 with respect to this matter.[93] Among other things, in General Comment No. 14 the Committee indicates how the best interests of children should be assessed and then determined and taken into account in decision making and legal procedures. The General Comment explains that the best interests of children must be examined and determined in each *individual case* in light of the *specific circumstances* of each child or each group of children. These circumstances are related to the *individual characteristics* of the child or group of children concerned, including the *social and cultural context* in which the child or group of children find themselves (italics added).[94]

This article discusses how the best interests of the child, based on a multidisciplinary pedagogic, developmental psychology and judicial approach, should be assessed and determined. The theoretical framework presented can be used for assessing and determining the best interests of the child in decision-making procedures in different (legal) situations where a child might be involved. This article presents the separate pedagogy, child psychology, as well as the concept of the best interests of the child from a combined child developmental and children's rights perspective. It also introduces the BIC model and BIC questionnaire, an interdisciplinary tool to assess the child's best interests on the basis of combined pedagogical, child developmental and legal principles. The article equally discusses the assessment of the child's best interests in accordance with General Comment No. 14.

93. UN Committee on the Rights of the Child, General Comment No. 14 (2013) on the right of the child to have his or her best interests taken as a primary consideration (Article 3.1).
94. General Comment No. 14 (2013), paragraph 48.

The best interests of the child from a pedagogy, child psychology and children's rights perspective

Pedagogy is a normative science: its central issues are the purpose of raising and educating children as well as what characterises a good upbringing and education. "Normative" means that there is a vision or idea about what is desirable in parenting and education, and this vision serves as an ideal objective. Child psychology focuses on the development of children and their needs, especially if the development is disturbed and child-rearing is problematic. This may be due to factors associated with the personality and behaviour of the child, the vulnerability, behavioural problems, personalities and other problems of the parents (which may mean that they do not have sufficient resources to protect their child and provide good parenting), or problems related to both the child and the parents. In practice, the priority of child psychologists and child-rearing specialists is the best interests of the child.[95] Child-rearing is not limited to the unique relationship between the parents and the child; it also takes place within the broader cultural and social context of the community. To a large extent, this context determines the normative framework according to which children are brought up. If the conditions in the community in which the child is reared are unfavourable, this can make child-rearing more difficult and jeopardise the child's development.

In the Netherlands, over the past 150 years, the influence of the government on child-rearing has increased steadily. Whereas before the Enlightenment child-rearing was mainly an individual matter for the parents and was closely linked to the religion of the parents in question, later the emphasis shifted to bringing up children to be good citizens, while aiming for the best possible development of those children.[96] The government's role in child-rearing was formalised in the child legislation which took effect in 1905 in the Netherlands. The government acts as a regulator of good parenting and a protector of developing children. If children go astray or their development is threatened because of failed parenting or a lack of safety, the government intervenes.

Children can also be placed under supervision. This means that the authority of the parents is limited or sometimes even taken away. In the Netherlands the Child Care and Protection Board plays a prominent role in this. The board examines whether the child's development and safety are endangered and advises the family courts or juvenile courts as to whether an intervention in parental authority is needed to safeguard the child's development and protect his or her rights. When assessing the case, the courts will examine whether the best interests of the child are served by the proposed decision. Not only in the Netherlands, but also in other western countries, there are government bodies which monitor the development and safety of children. International developments have also been a decisive factor in relation to the role of the government as a guardian and protector of children. After the Second World War many orphaned children all over the world were in need of protection, and the influence of the international community on our views of child-rearing increased steadily.

---

95. NVO (2008), *De Beroepscode van de NVO*, Nederlandse Vereniging van pedagogen en Onderwijskundigen, Utrecht, p. 9.
96. Fila J., Dekker J.J.H. and Wildschut Y. (eds.) (2013), *De kunst van het opvoeden*, WalburgPers, Zutphen.

The United Nations have played a major role in this development. With the UNCRC, a global normative legal framework for children's rights came into being in 1989. This framework focuses on the obligations of states to protect the well-being of children and to safeguard their development. The Committee on the Rights of the Child monitors whether states comply with the convention. The Committee regularly examines the children's rights situation in the countries which are party to the convention. In its concluding observations the Committee makes recommendations to these states for improvements in their policy.

European legislation, regulations and policy should be based on the fundamental principles of the UNCRC. These fundamental principles are determined by the four core articles of the convention: Article 2 (non-discrimination), Article 3 (the best interests of the child as a primary consideration), Article 6 (right to life and development) and Article 12 (right to be heard). These articles must be read together, and they constitute a frame of reference for the application of the rest of the provisions of the convention.

The interests of the child from an interdisciplinary perspective based on pedagogy, child development and children's rights

To arrive at an interdisciplinary "best interests of the child" perspective, the principles of child-rearing expertise and of children's rights have to be combined. This has led to the following results. The best interests of the child (Article 3) are those which favour the child's holistic development to adulthood (Article 6) within the cultural and social context of the community in which the child is growing up. The child must be able to have a say in decisions which affect him or her (Article 12) and must be treated in the same way as other children (Article 2). The child's upbringing is complete when he or she has developed to adulthood and can claim a place in society. The child has then been brought up to be a good citizen.

However, this picture is not yet complete. Grietens draws attention to a normative concept which stresses that bringing up children is not only about their development to adulthood, but also about the experience of childhood itself. Childhood is seen as an independent, intrinsically relevant and important stage of human life. The experiences and stories of children are significant in themselves and should not be considered only from a growth perspective.[97] If we examine the UNCRC in this light, we find several provisions which stress the value of childhood, such as Article 31 on the right to leisure and recreation and Article 10 on family reunification. This is why the normative framework of children's best interests is expanded by adding the right to and the need for a good childhood. To experience a good childhood and to develop in a positive way, a child needs a social context which provides opportunities to do so.

It is up to child development and child-rearing specialists in the fields of child psychology, special needs education and youth care studies to help develop theories

---

97. Grietens H. (2011), *Kleine stemmen, grote verhalen!? Over pleegkinderen in orthopedagogisch on derzoek*, Garant, Antwerpen/Apeldoorn.

and methods to support the child-rearing and education of vulnerable children. The children in question are those whose interests, both with regard to their childhood itself and to their development towards good citizenship, are threatened because of problems during their childhood relating to their upbringing and their prospects for the future within the cultural and social context in which they are growing up. One situation in which these specialists make this contribution is in relation to legal proceedings involving decisions which may affect children's lives. In these proceedings the best interests of children must be a primary consideration, children must receive equal treatment, and their views must be taken seriously.

The Best Interests of the Child model (the BIC model): an interdisciplinary perspective

To experience a good childhood and to develop in a positive way to become an adult and a good citizen, the child needs a social context which provides opportunities to do so. The Best Interests of the Child model, the BIC model, was developed in a joint project by Kalverboer and Zijlstra.[98] The BIC model builds on the list of 12 conditions for optimal development posited by Heiner and Bartels. Heiner and Bartels took these 12 conditions for development from an international literature review concerning children and the development of delinquent behaviour. According to these authors, it is in the interests of children to be able to develop well. To do so they need a social context which makes this possible.[99]

The BIC model developed by Kalverboer and Zijlstra consists of 14 child-rearing conditions in a child's life which must be of sufficiently high quality to enable children to experience a good childhood and to safeguard their development (see Figure 1). Together they represent the quality of the child-rearing environment.[100] If these conditions are of a sufficiently high standard during an extended period – both in the current situation and in the past and future – it can be said that there is continuity and stability in the child's upbringing and circumstances. This is in the best interests of the child. The child can develop and lives in a qualitatively good social environment. If these conditions are of an insufficient quality over an extended period, this may harm the child's development and their experience of their childhood. This applies particularly to vulnerable children.[101] The rearing environment of vulnerable children should meet extra high criteria.

98. Kalverboer, M.E. and Zijlstra, A.E. (2006), *Kinderen uit asielzoekersgezinnen en het recht op ontwikkeling: Het belang van het kind in het Vreemdelingenrecht*, SWP Publishers, Amsterdam.
99. Heiner J. and Bartels A.A.J. (1989), "Jeugdstrafrecht en het belang van het kind: Het belang van het kind nader omschreven", *Tijdschrift voor Familie- en Jeugdrecht*, 11, pp. 59–67.
100. Zijlstra A.E., *In the Best Interest of the Child. A study into a decision-support tool validating asylum-seeking children's rights from a behavioural scientific perspective*, Proefschrift, Groningen: Rijksuniversiteit Groningen, 2012, pp. 47–49.
101. Caprara G.V. and Rutter M (1995), "Individual development and social change", in M. Rutter and D.J. Smith (eds.), *Psychological disorders in young people: Time, trends and their causes*, John Wiley and Sons Ltd., Chichester, pp. 35-66.

Figure 1: The BIC model

Family: current situation

Physical well-being

1. Adequate physical care

Adequate physical care refers to the care for the child's health and physical well-being by parents or care providers. They offer the child a place to live, clothing to wear, enough food to eat and (some) personal belongings. There is a family income to provide for all this. In addition, the parents or care providers are free of worries about providing for the child's physical well-being.

2. Safe immediate physical environment

A safe direct physical environment offers the child physical protection. This implies the absence of physical danger in the house or neighbourhood in which the child lives. There are no toxins or other threats in the house or neighbourhood. The child is not threatened by abuse of any kind.

Care and upbringing

3. Affective atmosphere

An affective atmosphere implies that the parents or care providers of the child offer the child emotional protection, support and understanding. There are bonds of attachment between the parent(s) or caregiver(s) and the child. There is a relationship of mutual affection.

4. Supportive, flexible parenting structure

A supportive, flexible child-rearing structure encompasses several aspects such as:
- enough daily routine in the child's life;
- encouragement, stimulation and instruction to the child and the requirement of realistic demands;
- rules, limits, instructions and insight into why they are needed;
- control of the child's behaviour;
- enough space for the child's own wishes and thoughts, enough freedom to experiment and to negotiate over what is important to the child;
- no more responsibilities than the child is capable of handling (in this way the child learns the consequences of his or her behaviour within the limits which the parents or care providers have set).

5. Adequate example set by parents

The parents or care providers offer the child the opportunity to incorporate their behaviour, values and cultural norms that are important, now and in the future.

6. Interest in the child

The parents or care providers are attentive to the activities and interests of the child, and to his or her perception of the world.

Family: future and past

7. Continuity in upbringing and care, future perspective

The parents or care providers care for the child and bring the child up in such a way that attachment bonds develop. Basic trust is to be maintained by the availability of the parents or care providers to the child. The child has a future perspective.

Society: current situation

8. Safe wider physical environment

The neighbourhood the child grows up in is safe, as well as the society the child lives in. Criminality, (civil) wars, natural disasters, infectious diseases, etc. do not threaten the development of the child.

9. Respect

The needs, wishes, feelings and desires of the child are taken seriously by the child's environment and the society the child lives in. There is no discrimination because of background, race or religion.

10. Social network

The child and his or her family have various sources of support in their environment upon which they can depend.

11. Education

The child receives a suitable education and has the opportunity to develop his or her personality and talents (for example, sport or music).

12. Contact with peers and friends

The child has opportunities to have contact with other children in various situations suitable to his or her perception of the world and developmental age.

13. Adequate examples set by the community

The child is in contact with children and adults who are examples for current and future behaviour and who mediate the adaptation of important societal values and norms.

Society: future and past

14. Stability in life circumstances, future perspective

The environment in which the child is brought up does not change suddenly and unexpectedly. There is continuity in life circumstances. Significant changes are prepared for and made comprehensible for the child. Persons with whom the child can identify and sources of support are constantly available to the child, as well as the possibility of developing relationships by means of a common language. Society offers the child opportunities and a future perspective.

The BIC model and General Comment No. 14

The BIC model is consistent with the vision of the Committee on the Rights of the Child. The 14 child-rearing conditions of the BIC model together represent the social and cultural context the child grows up in. If the child-rearing conditions of the BIC model are of a sufficiently high quality over an extended period, there will be continuity and stability in the child's life; the child will be able to develop in a positive way.[102]

Conversely, if the conditions are of an insufficient quality over an extended period, this may harm the child's development and his or her experience of childhood; the child's identity will be threatened.[103] This applies particularly to vulnerable children. The rearing environment of vulnerable children should meet extra high criteria.[104] To experience a good childhood and to develop in a positive way, the child needs a social and cultural context which provides opportunities to do so. Good education, social bonds, ties with family and significant others, safety and respect for the child's individuality are essential.[105] Figure 2 shows which paragraphs of the General Comment No. 14 refer to the specific conditions identified in the BIC model as essential elements in the assessment and determination of the best interests of the child.

Figure 2: The BIC model with references to specific UNCRC articles and to the paragraphs of General Comment No. 14.[106]

	BIC conditions	UNCRC provisions which could be violated if the condition is of inadequate quality	Paragraphs of General Comment No. 14 in which an element is referred to
	Current situation		
	1. Adequate physical care	24, 26, 27	70, 77, 78, 84
	2. Safe immediate physical environment	19, 24	70, 71, 73, 74, 77, 78, 84
	3. Affective atmosphere	19	70, 71, 72, 84
	4. Supportive flexible parenting structure	13, 14	71, 84
	5. Adequate examples set by parents	10	71, 84
	6. Interest in the child	31	71, 84

---

102. See for instance General Comment No. 14 (2013), paragraph 84.
103. General Comment No. 14 (2013), paragraphs 55-56.
104. General Comment No. 14 (2013), paragraphs 75-76.
105. General Comment No. 14 (2013), paragraphs 48, 58-70, 71-74 and 79.
106. Kalverboer M.E. (2014), *The best interest of the child in migration law: significance and implications in terms of child development and child rearing*, SWP Publishers, Amsterdam, p. 16.

	Past and future		
	7. Continuity in upbringing and care, future perspective	5, 6, 9, 10, 18	58, 59, 60, 61, 62, 63, 65, 66, 67, 70, 72, 84
	Current situation		
	8. Safe wider physical environment	33, 34, 35, 36, 37	70, 71, 73, 74, 84
	9. Respect	2, 13, 14, 15, 16, 30, 37	56, 73, 74, 84
	10. Social network		70, 84
	11. Education	17, 28, 29, 31	79, 84
	12. Contact with peers and friends	31	70, 84
	13. Adequate examples set by the community	2, 8, 13, 14, 15	73, 84
	Past and future		
	14. Stability in life circumstances, future perspective	6, 9, 10, 20	65, 70, 72, 84

The BIC questionnaire: an interdisciplinary tool to assess the best interests of the child on the basis of developmental and legal principles

To assess the best interests of the child in decision-making procedures, Kalverboer and Zijlstra developed the BIC questionnaire (BIC-Q). The BIC model and BIC-Q can be used in all kinds of decisions, within all areas of law in which the best interests of the child shall be a primary consideration and in which the quality of the child's environment is in question.

The BIC-Q consists of 24 questions relating to the 14 child-rearing conditions. These 24 questions are answered in relation to (a) the child's current child-rearing and living situation, (b) the expected future situation if the current child-rearing and living situation continues, and (c) the expected future situation if an alternative child-rearing and living situation is chosen. A professional can therefore use the questionnaire to assess the child's current environment and to compare it with the situation which can be expected as the result of a specific decision. For each condition the professional can also assess which articles of the UNCRC are violated if the quality of a specific condition is inadequate (see Figure 2).

In her study, Zijlstra shows that there is correlation between the quality of the child-rearing environment in which a child grows up and the problems the child experiences.[107] This means that the BIC-Q scores can be used to make a prediction

107. Zijlstra A.E., In the Best Interest of the Child.

about the child's prospects for development if a specific decision were to be made. The questionnaire is used in combination with other assessment tools which explore the child's individual characteristics, such as the social and emotional state and vulnerability. In accordance with decision-making rules based on the key articles of the UNCRC, the alternative which offers the child the best childhood and the best opportunities for development should be chosen.

Assessment of the child's best interests in different legal situations in accordance with General Comment No. 14

According to the Committee on the Rights of the Child, to arrive at an adequate assessment of best interests, first of all the relevant elements in the best-interests assessment must be determined. The following elements must always be considered in the assessment: the child's views; the child's characteristics; preservation of the family environment and the child's relationships; care, protection and safety for the child; the child's vulnerability; the child's right to be heard and the child's right to education. In addition, there are elements which are specifically related to the individual situation of the child or group of children in question and the kind of decision that is being made. The elements must be *defined* and *assigned a relative weight*. A procedure must be followed which ensures *legal guarantees* and *proper application of the right* (italics mine).[108]

The best interests of the child must therefore be determined in each individual case; assessment takes place in the light of the specific circumstances of each child. Those making a decision must take the child's developmental possibilities into account. This means that not only the child's needs at the specific time of the decision should be determined, but also that the possible scenarios of the child's development should be considered and analysed in the long and short term. In this context, decisions should assess the continuity and stability of the child's present and future situations. Moreover, the best interests of the child must be determined by professionals, preferably by a multidisciplinary team. A best-interests assessment can only comply with the principles and intentions of Article 3 UNCRC if the child is heard and the child's views are taken into account in the best-interests assessment, and appropriate weight is given to them.[109]

Depending on the procedure the child is involved in, specific characteristics of the child are more or less important in the assessment of the child's best interests. To obtain the information necessary for a good impression of the child's characteristics, such as his or her identity, vulnerability and developmental prospects in relation to the decision to be made, the child is interviewed and observed in a child-friendly setting. In addition, in the assessment specific diagnostic methods and instruments are used depending on the particular decision to be made.

---

108. General Comment No. 14 (2013), paragraphs 46–79.
109. General Comment No. 14 (2013), paragraph 47.

To assess the social and cultural context of the child in specific decision-making procedures, the BIC questionnaire can be used.[110] A professional can use the questionnaire to assess the child's current environment and compare it with the situation which can be expected to arise if a specific decision is made.[111] With the BIC-Q, the professional can also determine which articles of the UNCRC are violated if the quality of a specific condition is inadequate (see Figure 2).

In the BIC self-report, a child or adolescent can indicate in which environment he or she prefers to grow up and which environment in his or her views provides the best opportunities for life and development (Article 12 UNCRC). This is the environment which according to the child or adolescent best serves his or her interests.[112]

Based on the assessment, a social welfare report is written. The report contains a description of how the child is developing, which problems the child faces in the current social and cultural context in which he or she is growing up and what prospects might be foreseen in relation to the different possible solutions available. In addition, the child's views on his or her best interests are written down in the report. In accordance with the decision-making rules based on the key articles in the UNCRC, the solution that offers the child the best childhood and the best opportunities for development should be chosen if the child's best interests are paramount.[113] This solution is recommended in the social welfare report as serving the child's best interests in the decision-making procedure.

Since in every decision-making procedure other interests are also involved, the child's best interests have to be balanced against these other interests. In the determination process, it is the task of the decision maker to balance these interests in the particular procedure involving the child. Procedural guarantees should ensure that assessment and determination are correctly implemented.

The reliability and validity of the BIC-Q have been established for migration procedures involving children and put into practice in individual cases of children involved in asylum and immigration procedures in the Netherlands.[114] The reliability and validity of the BIC-Q have also been established in the field of domestic and juvenile law. The BIC-Q seems to be a reliable and valid measure of the overall quality of child-rearing and may be applied to support court decisions on where a child should live after detention or secure placement.[115]

110. Kalverboer M.E. and Zijlstra A.E. (2006), *Het belang van het kind in het Nederlands recht: voorwaarden voor ontwikkeling vanuit een pedagogisch perspectief*, SWP Publishers, Amsterdam; Kalverboer M.E., Ten Brummelaar M.D.C., Post W.J.M., Zijlstra A.E., Harder A.T. and Knorth E.J. (2012), "The Best Interest of the Child Questionnaire, reliability and validity: Preliminary data on the question 'where to live after detention or secure treatment?'", *Criminal Behaviour and Mental Health*, 22 (1),41-52; Zijlstra A.E., *In the Best Interest of the Child*.
111. General Comment No. 14 (2013), paragraph 84.
112. Ten Brummelaar M.D.C., Kalverboer M.E., Harder A.T., Post W.J., Zijlstra A.E. and Knorth E.J. (2014), "The Best Interest of the Child Self-report questionnaire (BIC-S): Results of a participatory development procedure", *Child Indicators Research*, 7; General Comment No. 14 (2013), paragraphs 43-44 and 89.
113. General Comment No. 14 (2013), paragraphs 43-44 and 84.
114. Kalverboer M.E., *The best interest of the child in migration law*; Zijlstra, A.E., *In the Best Interest of the Child*.
115. Kalverboer M.E., et. al (2012), "The Best Interest of the Child Questionnaire", pp. 41-52.

Closing remarks

In conclusion, General Comment No. 14 offers transparent guidelines for assessing and determining the child's best interests. If these guidelines are followed, the key principles of the UNCRC will have a significant place in decisions. The different elements of the assessment should be carefully selected and the content of these elements carefully determined. The different interests should be carefully balanced to facilitate a transparent decision. The full and effective enjoyment of children's rights should form the basis of this decision. A decision that is in accordance with General Comment No. 14 not only takes account of the child's current interests but will also estimate what the future consequences of the decision will be for the child's life and holistic development. Whenever possible family ties and contacts with significant others should be preserved. By following the guidelines of the General Comment, children's rights will be fully protected in decision-making procedures involving children.

The BIC model and the BIC questionnaire are in accordance with General Comment No. 14 and can be used as tools in the assessment and determination of the child's best interests in all kinds of legal and other decision-making procedures in which the quality of child-rearing – the social and cultural context the child grows up in – is at stake.

The best interests of the child assessment with recently arrived refugee children

Carla van Os[116]
Study Centre for Children, Migration and Law, University of Groningen, faculty of behavioural and social sciences

In 2014, the United Nations Convention on the Rights of the Child (UNCRC) celebrated its 25th anniversary. While the best interests of the child have for a much longer time been a major concern for professionals working with children, the UNCRC gave children the legal right to have their best interests assessed and used as a primary consideration when decisions concerning them are taken. In order to safeguard the best interests of children it is important to have scientific standards for the way the best of interests of the child should be assessed. The contribution of Margrite Kalverboer in this publication (Chapter 2.2) shows how a specific model, the Best Interests of the Child model (BIC model), can provide such a standard. In this text, I discuss applying the BIC model to refugee children as well as relevant factors that should be involved in the best interests of the child assessment for the first decision in the migration procedure.

The BIC model consists of 14 pedagogical and environmental conditions that promote and should safeguard the development of the child.[117] The right to development, safeguarded by Article 6 of the UNCRC, is closely linked to the best interests concept safeguarded by Article 3 of the convention. Moreover, states have the obligation to ensure the right to development in the assessment of the best interests of the child.[118]

---

116. Contact: e.c.c.van.os@rug.nl.
117. Kalverboer M.E. (2014), *The best interest of the child in migration law: significance and implications in terms of child development and child rearing*, SWP, Amsterdam; Kalverboer M.E. and Zijlstra A.E. (2006), *Kinderen uit asielzoekersgezinnen en het recht op ontwikkeling: Het belang van het kind in het Vreemdelingenrecht* (The interests of the child in Dutch law: Conditions of child development from a pedagogigal perspective), SWP Publishers, Amsterdam; Zijlstra A. E. (2012), *In the best interest of the child; a study into a decision-support tool validating asylum-seeking children's rights from a behavioural scientific perspective* (diss.) Groningen: University of Groningen.
118. UN Committee on the Rights of the Child, General Comment No. 14 (2013) on the right of the child to have his or her best interests taken as a primary consideration (Article 3.1), paragraph 42.

The BIC model reflects different aspects listed in General Comment No. 14 of the United Nations Committee on the Rights of the Child concerning the implementation of the best interests of the child principle.[119] The Committee recognises both the individual characteristics of the child (identity and vulnerability) and the socio-cultural context in which the child lives among essential pillars of the best interests of the child assessment[120] and highlights the importance of conducting a careful best-interests assessment and determination in every situation.

For refugee children[121] arriving in the host country, an assessment of the best interests of the child and determination have to be made. Decision making in a migration procedure obliges the decision makers to gather a lot of information on an unknown – recently arrived – child and requires them to be able to interpret this information in a way which corresponds with the principle of the best interests of the child.

Research on newly[122] arrived refugee children has shown that it is important to know which and how many stressful life events a child has experienced before arrival in the host country[123] as well as the duration and severity of these events.[124] Relevant experiences that should be taken into account in this process are exposure to violence,[125] separation and loss of close relatives,[126] feelings of being in danger prior to and during the flight,[127] family situational changes,[128] physical maltreatment,[129]

119. General Comment No. 14 (2013), paragraphs 58-74.
120. General Comment No. 14 (2013), paragraph 48.
121. This paper focuses on both unaccompanied children and children who are accompanied by (one of) their parents or care givers, who are forced to leave their home country in search of protection in another country. In most cases, these children ask for asylum and can therefore be defined in a legal sense as asylum-seeking children. Legally, these children are called refugees once their asylum claim has been accepted. Working from a pedagogical point of view, I prefer to call these children refugees: seeking protection either on the grounds of being a refugee in the sense of the 1951 Refugee Convention or because of other forms of perceived danger in the home country.
122. The literature referred to in this paragraph deals with research on refugee children who were less than one year in the host country.
123. Jensen T.K., Fjermestad K.W., Granly L., and Wilhelmsen N.H. (2013), "Stressful life experiences and mental health problems among unaccompanied asylum-seeking children", Clinical Child Psychology and Psychiatry, 20(1), pp. 106-116.; Montgomery E. (1998), "Refugee children from the Middle East", Scandinavian Journal of Social Medicine, Supplementum, 54, pp. 1-152.; Vervliet M., Meyer Demott M. A., Jakobsen M., Broekaert E., Heir T. and Derluyn I. (2014), "The mental health of unaccompanied refugee minors on arrival in the host country", Scandinavian Journal of Psychology, 55(1), pp. 33-37.
124. Abdallah K., and Elklit A. (2001), "A nationwide screening survey of refugee children from Kosovo", Torture, 11(2), pp. 45-49; Almqvist K. and Brandell-Forsberg M. (1997), "Refugee children in Sweden: Post-traumatic stress disorder in Iranian preschool children exposed to organized violence", Child Abuse and Neglect, 21(4), pp. 351–366.
125. Ekblad S. (1993), "Psychosocial adaptation of children while housed in a Swedish refugee camp: Aftermath of the collapse of Yugoslavia", Stress Medicine, 9(3), pp. 159-166.; Montgomery (1998); Rothe E., Lewis J., Castillo-Matos H., Martinez O., Busquets R. and Martinez I. (2002), "Posttraumatic stress disorder among Cuban children and adolescents after release from a refugee camp", Psychiatric Services, 53(8), pp. 970-976.
126. Montgomery (1998).
127. Abdallah and Elklit (2001); Rothe et al. (2002).
128. Abdallah and Elklit (2001); Montgomery (1998).
129. Abdallah and Elklit (2001); Geltman P.L., Augustyn M., Barnett, E.D., Klass P.E. and Groves B.M. (2000), "War trauma experience and behavioral screening of Bosnian refugee children resettled in Massachusetts", Journal of Developmental and Behavioral Pediatrics, 21(4), pp. 255-261; Montgomery (1998).

extreme poverty[130] and the circumstances of life in a refugee camp outside the home country.[131] The most common mental health problems children face upon arrival are post-traumatic stress disorder, depression and several anxiety disorders.[132] The assessment of the vulnerability of the child[133] is also necessary for the assessment of the quality of the rearing environment. The more vulnerable the child is, the higher the qualifications of the family and social environment have to be in order to guarantee a safe and good development of the child.[134]

The 14 conditions for development in the BIC model should be assessed for each child that asks for international protection.[135] For both recently arrived unaccompanied and accompanied children, the situation prior to flight is crucial in the best interests of the child assessment, since that is where the child will return to in case his or her request for protection is rejected. After the assessment of the first six family conditions for development it is important to assess in which environment the continuity and stability in the upbringing is safeguarded (condition 7, BIC model). In the situation of a refugee child, it should be assessed what the deportation of the child to the home country would mean for the way the parents or care givers are able to provide the child with a good rearing environment.

For refugee children, almost by definition, a safe environment in a broader social context (condition 8, BIC model) is endangered due to conflicts in the home country. Not only the direct exposure to violence but also the continuous stressful threat that people have to live with in war situations may endanger the healthy development of the child.[136] For refugee children, the feeling of (not) being respected by society (condition 9, BIC model) is often related to the condition of safety.[137] The last condition (14) in the BIC model refers again to continuity and stability. When the previous six conditions in society at the moment before departure are assessed, it is important to know how these conditions will be fulfilled in the future when a decision about a child is taken in the asylum procedure.

Interviewers in the decision-making procedure should be aware that the traumatic experiences might hamper the ability of refugee children to tell their story in a

130. Abdallah and Elklit (2001).
131. Montgomery (1998).
132. Abdallah and Elklit (2001); Almqvist and Brandell-Forsberg (1997); Goldin S., Levin L., Persson L.A. and Hägglof B.(2001), "Stories of pre-war, war and exile: Bosnian refugee children in Sweden", *Medicine, Conflict, and Survival*, 17(1), pp. 25-47; Jakobsen M., Demott M.A.M. and Heir T. (2014), "Prevalence of psychiatric disorders among unaccompanied asylum-seeking adolescents in Norway", *Clinical Practice and Epidemiology in Mental Health*, 10, pp. 53–58.; Jensen et al. (2013); Sourander A. (1998), "Behavior problems and traumatic events of unaccompanied refugee minors", *Child Abuse and Neglect*, 22(7), pp. 719-727; Vervliet et al. (2014).
133. General Comment No. 14 (2013), paragraphs 75-76.
134. Caprara G. V. and Rutter M. (1995), "Individual development and social change", in Rutter M. and Smith D. J. (eds.), *Psychological disorders in young people: Time, trends and their causes*, Chichester: John Wiley & Sons Ltd, pp. 35-66.
135. For the definitions of the conditions, see the contribution of Kalverboer in this publication, Chapter 2.2.
136. Montgomery (1998).
137. Goldin et al. (2001).

coherent and consistent manner.[138] Apart from the effect of traumatic experiences, interviewers of refugee children may meet additional difficulties as a result of mistrust and its subsequent silence, which are often seen among young refugees.[139]

In conclusion, a decision about the child's need for international protection should be based on the child's right to development, similarly to the way the right to development is being applied in child protection law. If a child's development is at risk in his or her current living situation in the home country, the state authorities have an obligation to intervene in order to safeguard the safety and development of the child (Articles 6 and 19 UNCRC). Especially for recently arrived refugee children, it is necessary to assess whether their development was endangered before they fled and, if so, whether the perspectives on improvement of these conditions for development are guaranteed in case the child returns.

---

138. UNHCR (2014), *The heart of the matter. Assessing credibility when children apply for asylum in the European Union*, United Nations High Commissioner for Refugees, Brussels.
139. Kohli R.S. (2006), "The sound of silence: Listening to what unaccompanied asylum-seeking children say and do not say", *British Journal of Social Work*, 36(5), pp. 707-721; Ní Raghallaigh M. (2014), "The causes of mistrust amongst asylum seekers and refugees: Insights from research with unaccompanied asylum-seeking minors living in the Republic of Ireland", *Journal of Refugee Studies*, 27(1), pp. 82-100.

Monitoring best-interests decisions – Can systems developed for monitoring return decisions serve as an inspiration for other domains?[140]

Hanne Op de Beeck
Assistant-director at the research department of the Flemish Community Commission, former Senior Research and Policy Advice Officer, Children's Rights Knowledge Centre

Although monitoring is an important part of a best-interests decision-making process, it is currently lacking in decisions of this kind.[141] The value of monitoring and evaluation after a decision is taken primarily lies in their potential to instigate a learning process. Feedback can be highly informative for the decision maker, since it stimulates the development of knowledge and expertise based on which future decisions can be improved.[142] Moreover, evaluation of the outcomes of a decision can advance the quality of a decision altogether. Knowing that the expected outcomes will later be compared with the actual outcomes of a decision may not only lead to better quality assessments by the decision maker, it can also facilitate the identification of possible methodological errors.[143] Furthermore, public control as well as possibilities for appeal are basic conditions for a democratic process. Therefore, monitoring is an important part of a democratic best-interests decision.[144]

---

140. This text is inspired by a workshop held in the European Conference on the Best Interests of the Child in Brussels in December 2014. The issues, challenges and recommendations discussed are based on the concerns that were brought forward together with the participants of the workshop.
141. Op de Beeck H., Herbots K., Lembrechts S., Willems N. and Vlieghe K. (2014), *Children's best interests between theory and practice. A discussion of commonly encountered tensions and possible solutions based on international best interests practices and policy strategies since 2004*, Kenniscentrum Kinderrechten vzw, Ghent, p. 60.
142. Op de Beeck et al. (2014), *Children's best interests between theory and practice*, p. 60.
143. Ibid.
144. Ibid.

It is remarkable that the most extensive monitoring initiatives regarding best-interests decisions have been developed in the domain of migration.[145] For instance the HIT Foundation, a foundation developing solutions to tackle challenges related to migration, has developed a monitoring system to follow up on return decisions affecting minors.[146] The goal of this project, which was commissioned by the European Commission, was to come up with a safer and more sustainable system for the return of minors, based on the principle of best interests. In addition to the initiative of the HIT Foundation, there are other examples of monitoring initiatives regarding best-interests decisions that have been developed in the domain of migration. The Finnish Assisted Voluntary Return programme includes in return decisions a clear integration and monitoring system as well as protection for parent(s) or guardian(s) in the home country. The Spanish reunification programme monitors assisted returns of children, the effective reunification with the family and/or the availability of adequate care for the child.[147]

Different explanations are possible for this focus on migration. As immigrant children often find themselves in a situation that is especially precarious and as they form a target group that is difficult to reach monitoring may be more crucial in their case. Also the fact that – at least for unaccompanied migrant minors – parents or guardians, who are usually responsible for taking the decisions that may largely affect the child's life, are completely absent and therefore cannot even be heard, may more strongly necessitate monitoring of the decisions taken.[148]

The question here is to what extent these monitoring systems for return decisions could serve as a model to be expanded to other best interests decisions. The HIT example shows that monitoring systems for return decisions can at the very least inspire a broader discussion on what monitoring of best interests decisions in general should look like.[149] Frans Bastiaens, the director of the HIT Foundation, presented at the European Conference on the Best Interests of the Child the situation of 150 migrant minors residing in EU countries who were – forcefully or voluntarily – returned to their home countries Kosovo and Albania. Based on the HIT monitoring instrument, it was found that 37% of these children suffered from social and emotional problems and were in need of psychological treatment after their return. Growing up in poverty, the lack of an affective home climate, the lack of schooling and of friends and social networks are risk factors that add to these problems. These findings illustrate monitoring's potential to inspire asylum and return policies that are more tailored to the needs of these returning minors. Furthermore, the monitoring system can be used in individual asylum cases as well as it allows for better decision making and assistance for particular children.[150]

What could be done to improve monitoring and evaluation of best-interests decisions in general? Are monitoring and evaluation an obligation under the United Nations

145. Ibid.
146. Bastiaens F., "Monitoring of Returned Children", paper presented at the European Conference on the Best Interests of the Child, Brussels, 9-10 December 2014, p. 19.
147. Op de Beeck et al. (2014), *Children's best interests between theory and practice,* p. 60.
148. Ibid.
149. HIT Foundation, "Monitoring returned minors", unpublished report, 2014, p. 16.
150. Bastiaens (2014), "Monitoring of Returned Children", p. 19.

Convention on the Rights of the Child (UNCRC)? If so, to what extent is this obligation put into practice? It is clear that best interests cannot be ignored in migration.
An important challenge is related to the lack of knowledge and therefore a lack of
usage of the best interests concept among most immigration authorities as well as in
international immigration legislation. This void may cause some peculiar side effects.
One specific example of this is related to the sustainability of the best interests concept. Based on the best interests principle, a range of protective measures can shield
the child from a forced or detrimental return. However, most protection measures
traditionally end when the child reaches the age of majority, while by that age he
or she is likely to have become fully integrated in the new country. In that light, a
more sustainable or transitional way to deal with the best interests principle could be
beneficial. The duty for states to mainstream the best interests principle to different
policy domains, such as migration, should be included in Article 3 of the UNCRC.

When discussing monitoring of decisions related to best interests in general, different
levels of monitoring can be distinguished. One of them is monitoring at the general
level, which entails monitoring and evaluation in order to improve policies based on
the best interests principle. The second way of perceiving monitoring is monitoring
at the individual level, which could include, for instance, providing possibilities for
appeal in case an individual decision is contested.

A key question related to monitoring is who is responsible for creating and maintaining
a monitoring system. Is this a responsibility for states, or should non-governmental
organisations have a role as well? It seems reasonable that at least the responsibility for
establishing a monitoring system would lie with the states. Regarding return decisions,
however, there can be confusion as to which state should carry this responsibility:
is it the original home country of the child (the state the child was born or grew up
in)? Or should the receiving state organise monitoring and evaluation after having
processed a return decision? If this question was addressed in the frame that was
put forward by Op de Beeck et al. (2014), who argue that monitoring is a specifically
important part of a learning process which allows the decision maker to take more
appropriate decisions in the future, or Bastiaens (2014), who defines the adjustment
of return policies and decisions as one of the main benefits of monitoring, it appears
that it should be the receiving state who assumes this responsibility.

Another important concern is the implementation of the monitoring process.
Questions can be raised as to what extent states will be motivated to take up the
monitoring in a qualitative manner. Are there any possible ways of encouraging states
to do so? Different possibilities can be distinguished in this regard. Three of those
focus on appealing to the states themselves. First, the intrinsic motivation of the
states should be addressed. Creating a sound follow-up process would allow them
to evaluate the efficiency and quality of their own policies. In the end, this would
not only benefit the individual children but also the state as a whole. The second
option would be to enforce qualitative monitoring and evaluation by the states. For
example, the United Nations Committee on the Rights of the Child could request
states to include their efforts on monitoring in their reports. A third option would
be to create a mixed model in which states and non-governmental organisations
would do the monitoring together through a complementary system.

In addition to these possibilities, it could be beneficial to focus on creating an environment that promotes or facilitates monitoring. One way to do so would be appealing to the media since it can make the broader public more attentive to the importance of monitoring. By doing so, the public could follow up on the states' efforts to organise monitoring. Another way is to support improved data-collection and registration systems. Preferably, these systems should be aligned to one another.

In conclusion, it can be stated that a number of well-established systems already exist. One of these examples is the monitoring system in return decisions developed by the HIT Foundation. Even though such systems might be specifically designed for migration issues, they can at least serve as a source of inspiration or consultation to create sound monitoring structures for best interests decisions in other areas.

Even though the responsibility for monitoring appears to predominantly lie with the states, mixed models in which non-governmental organisations have a complementary role could be beneficial for the realisation and implementation of monitoring. To encourage states to take the initiative in setting up adequate monitoring systems, two approaches can be brought forward. These approaches could also be combined. First of all, a more "monitoring-friendly" atmosphere can generally be advocated through sensitising the broader public about best interests issues and the importance of monitoring (such as through the media) and through creating more qualitative registration systems that are comparable between countries. A second option is to directly appeal to the states themselves, either intrinsically by emphasising the value of monitoring or extrinsically by assigning the Committee to follow up on monitoring initiatives, for instance.

Finally, and most importantly, it should be underlined that monitoring is indispensable for quality best interests practices. The best interests of the child are inevitably a dynamic concept, therefore it is important to establish a dynamic decision-making process as well. Monitoring and evaluation can add to such a dynamic process, as they allow for the establishment of a learning process, the adaptation of policies and the revision of individual results. Thus, even though the reflections and recommendations discussed in this article may only touch the surface of monitoring issues, they can be considered as important first steps towards more extensive and well-supported decision-making structures.

Chapter 3

Best interests of the child in different environments

The concept of the child's best interests in the work of the Council of Europe

Regína Jensdóttir
*Head of the Children's Rights Division and the Council of Europe
Coordinator on Children's Rights*

Defining a child's best interests is a challenging endeavour. How many adults can even say what their own best interests are? All our decisions are essentially based on what we know at any given moment, and this knowledge is often limited and fails to factor in many other important aspects and constraints of our adult lives. We need to therefore acknowledge that we may never be able to actually define what is in our own best interests or, for that matter, what is in a child's best interests. The principle of the best interests of the child is inherently abstract and subjective, which is why I think we need to exercise a degree of humility when applying it.

Because of its abstract nature, the principle can be applied in many ways. It runs the risk of being referenced in contexts where it merely serves to show superficial consideration of children's rights or even to justify detrimental actions. It can be a powerful tool for defending any decision taken for or on behalf of children, even those which are clearly not in their best interests but in the best interests of someone else or even the state. The concept has evoked many critical voices over the years and it is easy to question the added value of such an undefined abstract principle. If used correctly, the principle can however serve as a tool for securing children's rights. In other words, if it is actually used 'in the best interests of the child'.

The Council of Europe is mindful of the limitations inherent in the principle of the best interests of the child. We have striven to find the right balance between giving it concrete substance and leaving sufficient room for interpretation for it to be applied to each individual situation. Since 1989, the Council of Europe has included the principle of the best interests of the child in many of its legal instruments in the area of children's rights, such as in the European Convention on the Exercise of Children's Rights, the European Convention on the Adoption of Children and the Lanzarote Convention on Protection of Children against Sexual Exploitation and

Sexual Abuse. In addition, Council of Europe bodies working on topics relating to children's rights have recognised the importance of taking the best interests of the child into account. The Venice Commission recently examined children's rights in the constitutions of Council of Europe member states to verify the direct and indirect effect of rights safeguarded by the United Nations Convention on the Rights of the Child (UNCRC). In its conclusions, the Commission even went so far as to recommend that states provide constitutional guarantees for the principle.

The principle of the best interests of the child has served many different functions in the work of the Council of Europe. The main functions of the principle are first combining rights; second, balancing rights; and third, guiding the implementation of rights. These three main functions are going to be addressed in the following.

The first main function served by the principle of the best interests of the child is that of combining rights. The principle of the best interests of the child can be used to assist in reinforcing existing rights of the child. An interesting example is the prohibition of corporal punishment. The UNCRC does not contain any provision explicitly prohibiting this form of punishment. The grounds for prohibition were achieved through the combined application of Article 19 of the UNCRC and the principle of the best interests of the child. Based on this joint application, the Council of Europe actively promotes the prohibition of corporal punishment in its member states. A full prohibition has now been enacted in over half of the Council of Europe member states. How could we have achieved this progress without referring to the best interests of the child principle, given that there is no direct legal prohibition of corporal punishment?

The Council of Europe Commissioner for Human Rights often uses the principle to *reinforce existing rights*. Through his recommendations, the Commissioner is giving substance to the principle by providing concrete guidance on what can in fact be considered in the best interests of the child. This is especially true for his work in the context of migrant children, where national legislation and procedures often lack appropriate measures for protecting them. He has stressed the importance of recognising that children are first of all children and that state authorities in Europe should always act with their best interests at heart. He has also fought to end the forced return of children to countries where their best interests may not be served. The Commissioner has also relied on the best interests principle in his fight against statelessness of children, stating that it is "clearly in the best interests of the child to have citizenship from birth" and that states should ensure that no child born on their territory is left stateless.[151]

The European Committee of Social Rights, the monitoring of the European Social Charter, believes that the personal scope of the Charter must be determined according to the child's best interests. The Committee has for example, on the basis of the best interests principle, extended the scope of certain rights contained in the Charter to children in irregular situations. Although the Charter normally only applies to nationals of contracting States or to those lawfully present on a State's territory, the

---

151. Council of Europe Commissioner for Human Rights, Human Rights Comment, "Governments should act in the best interest of stateless children", 15 January 2013.

Committee extended it to cover children who are in an irregular situation on the territory of a State based on the principle of the best interests of the child. This is an important development that may have been difficult to achieve without reference to the principle.

The second function of the best interests principle is to facilitate the *balancing* of rights. It is often necessary to balance rights that appear to be in conflict; a task that the European Court of Human Rights is often confronted with. The Court only has jurisdiction to review violations of the European Convention on Human Rights. Nonetheless, it has interpreted the Convention – which does not in itself refer to the concept of the best interests of the child – in line with Article 3 of the UNCRC. The court places much emphasis on the best interests of the child being the primary consideration. It has on many occasions taken note of the broad consensus in international law that the best interests of the child must be paramount in all actions concerning the child.[152]

The interests most often at stake in cases before the Court are those of the child, the parents and the public order. The interests at stake may also be in the form of conflicting rights that children themselves possess. In family cases for example, it may be on the one hand in the child's interests to maintain ties with his or her family and on the other, in the child's interests to be able to grow up outside his or her family environment. In such cases, the principle of the best interests of the child serves as guidance in striking the right balance between the various rights at stake, whether they be rights of different stakeholders or rights of the child itself.

The European Committee of Social Rights is also often faced with the balancing of conflicting rights. The Committee takes the principle of the best interests of the child into account when examining all issues relating to children's rights. In regard to the restriction of parental rights, the Committee considers for instance that any restrictions or limitations of parents' custodial rights should not go beyond what is necessary for the protection of the child's best interests and the rehabilitation of the family. In such cases, it may be difficult to come to a decision without using the principle of the best interests of the child as guidance.

The third function of the best interests principle is to *guide the implementation of rights*. It serves as an important principle of guidance when it comes to the implementation of existing measures in practice. Many bodies of the Council of Europe have referred to it in this context. The Committee for the Prevention of Torture and Inhuman or Degrading Treatment or Punishment (CPT) visits detention centres and investigates the circumstances in which children are deprived of liberty. The CPT's many country reports highlight the need to secure an appropriate environment for children in this extremely vulnerable situation. The CPT has also emphasised on the importance of maintaining contact between the child and his/her family. In its standards[153] it made an explicit reference to the best interests principle by stating that "taking into account the best interests of the child, the detention of a child can rarely be justified and that it can certainly not be motivated by lack of residence status".

---

152. See, for example, *X v. Latvia* [GC], *No. 27853/09*, paragraph 96, 23 November 2013; *Jeunesse v. the Netherlands* [GC], No. 12738/10, paragraph 118, 3 October 2014.
153. For CPT standards, see http://www.cpt.coe.int/en/documents/eng-standards.pdf.

By clearly stating what is considered to be in the child's best interests, the CPT uses the concept as a guiding principle for member states taking decisions concerning children deprived of liberty. All the efforts made by the CPT are essentially aimed at helping states secure the best interests of the child in their implementation of rights.

The Council of Europe Group of Experts on Action against Trafficking in Human Beings (GRETA) monitors the Council of Europe Convention on Action against Trafficking in Human Beings, which addresses the situation of trafficking of children in its country reports. The principle of the best interests of the child is frequently referenced in its reports and GRETA even provides states with guidance on what the principle entails in practice. GRETA considers "that any situation should be looked at from the child's own perspective, seeking to take the child's views into consideration and with the objective of ensuring that his/her rights are respected".[154] GRETA has also recently incorporated an entirely new focus on children in its questionnaire for the second evaluation round. States are now requested to answer detailed questions on how they secure the best interests of the child in relation to several issues concerning child victims of trafficking. The issues addressed include identification, the appointment of a legal guardian and the safe return of the child to its country of origin. By providing a definition of the best interests of the child and including it in specific questions, GRETA is ensuring that States effectively apply it.

The Lanzarote Convention on the Protection of Children against Sexual Exploitation and Sexual Abuse explicitly refers to the best interests of the child principle in numerous articles, in particular in the provisions dealing with investigations and criminal proceedings (child-friendly justice for example) and the protection of the child victim (such as removing the alleged perpetrator or the victim from his or her family environment or the need for therapeutic assistance to victims). The first implementation report of the Lanzarote Committee, monitoring body of the Convention, focuses on the protection of children against sexual abuse in the circle of trust. States parties were asked to specifically explain how the principle of the best interests of the child victim is enforced in this context. The Committee's findings concluded that in order for parties to guarantee the child victim's best interest, more attention should be paid to the rules, procedures, measures and settings which have proven to be effective in reducing the child's trauma. These included for example establishing or reinforcing close co-operation between competent bodies and professionals assigned to cases involving victims, to offer children the possibility of obtaining emotional support, or for parties to be able to choose between different options when having to protect the victim from his or her family environment. By analysing and comparing different protective measures and methods implemented by states parties, the Lanzarote Committee is able to bring forward promising practices which protect children and guarantee their best interests, all of which can be used by states as an inspiration when designing new policies.

The Committee of Ministers and the Parliamentary Assembly of the Council of Europe frequently refer to the principle in their recommendations and resolutions. The Guidelines of the Committee of Ministers on child-friendly justice, for example,

---

154. GRETA(2014)13. *Questionnaire for the evaluation of the implementation of the Council of Europe Convention on Action against Trafficking in Human Beings by parties: Second Evaluation round*, p. 5.

provide detailed guidance on how the principle of the best interests of the child shall be applied in judicial proceedings. The Council of Europe, together with the EU, has been working hard to promote these guidelines in the member states and aims to secure a more child-friendly justice system based on what is in the best interests of the child. The Committee of Ministers has also adopted a recommendation on the participation of children and young people under the age of 18. Participation is of course an important factor, necessary for the effective implementation of the best interests of the child.

In conclusion, the principle of the best interests of the child has added much considerable value to the work carried out by the Council of Europe. The Council of Europe is working in many different ways to promote the principle and guides its member states as to making a balanced application. However, as the principle is abstract and lends itself to many different applications according to the situation, it is difficult and certainly not recommended to establish a clear definition of what the principle encompasses. There is a need to preserve its flexibility, but there is of course also a need for an agreed determination procedure. The Council of Europe's core role is to set legal standards that are sufficiently clear for the legislator and the practitioner to apply, thereby guaranteeing that the child's best interests have been assessed and taken into account at all professional levels.

A debate on the best interests of the child is very much needed to develop the principle further and better ensure the effective enjoyment of children's human rights. The best interests of many children in Europe are not determined as they should, and it is our responsibility as adults to ensure that existing human rights legal frameworks are applied in practice and that the interests of others do not override the rights and interests of children.

The concept of the best interests of the child in the work of the European Union

Margaret Tuite
European Commission Coordinator for the rights of the child

The European Union, at the time of the adoption of its Charter of Fundamental Rights, sought to reflect the United Nations Convention on the Rights of the Child (UNCRC) focus on the best interests of the child in Article 24 of the Charter. Article 24 states that: "In all actions relating to children, whether taken by public authorities or private institutions, the child's best interests must be a primary consideration." As one can see, this formulation is almost identical word for word to the wording of Article 3.1 of the UNCRC. Article 24 also provides that "every child shall have the right to maintain on a regular basis a personal relationship and direct contact with both his or her parents, unless that is contrary to his or her interests."

The best interests of the child as a primary consideration is firmly embedded in several pieces of EU legislation, such as the 2003 Brussels IIa Regulation, Directive 2011/36/EU on trafficking in human beings, Directive 2011/93/EU combating the sexual abuse and sexual exploitation of children and child pornography, and Directive 2012/29/EU establishing minimum standards on the rights, support and protection of victims of crime, which states that the child's best interests must be assessed on an individual basis. Even Directive 2008/52/EC on mediation in civil and commercial matters, which does not include other provisions on children, provides for the confidentiality of mediators, except when required to ensure protection of the best interests of children. The Dublin III Regulation 604/2013, for example, sets out some criteria for a best-interests assessment, such as family reunification possibilities, the child's well-being and development, the views of the child in accordance with his or her age and level of maturity, safety and security considerations, especially with regard to a risk that the child may be a victim of trafficking.

Cross-border family conflicts are an area for which the European Commission and Parliament receive many queries and complaints. They are also clearly connected to the best interests of the child. Every year, thousands of children in the EU are affected by cross-border family conflicts. They often become involved in long legal disputes. In some cases, children may be abducted by one of their parents. These matters are covered by the Brussels IIa Regulation, a cornerstone in European family law and a building block of a common judicial area. It has now been applied for over 10 years. The principle of the best interests of the child is its primary consideration; the principle has been embedded in the regulation's recitals and numerous provisions, such as return of the child proceedings.

However, the experience and evaluation undertaken recently by the Commission show that the Brussels IIa Regulation falls short in ensuring swift and effective mechanisms for identifying courts, recognition and enforcement of judgments in cross-border situations. These shortcomings are particularly important given their impact on children and their rights as guaranteed by the Charter of Fundamental Rights.

A report on the application of Brussels IIa published in 2014 concluded that targeted improvements to the existing rules are needed. In summer 2014 a public consultation on the operation of the regulation was conducted. Replies from stakeholders, including member states and their judicial authorities, show that they understand and support the need for at least a carefully targeted reform of the regulation. This could cover the setting of common minimum standards for the hearing of the child, noting also that 78% of respondents to the consultation considered that this would be helpful. Furthermore, the review could include additional rules for fast return proceedings before the courts as well as the actual enforcement of the return order, to protect the child from the risk of parental abduction.

The concept of the best interests of the child is not without problems. We know there are risks of manipulation, and there is the risk that something so vague can result in back of an envelope assessments. There is a risk of what Nigel Cantwell suggests in this publication, that the concept has grown in importance well beyond the original intent.[155] In his text, Jorge Cardona Llorens suggests that assessments for the same situation for five different children potentially require five different decisions, but that individual assessments on the same child need to lead to the same result.[156] The best interests assessment should not be what the assessor considers to be the best, subjectively, but rather objectively whatever best guarantees comprehensive respect for all of the child's rights. In short, we need to proceed with caution.

Given the place of the best interests of the child principle now in EU law, it is useful to look at how member states implement it at national level. In our study to collect data on children's involvement in criminal, civil and administrative judicial proceedings, we sought to collect data on how member states of the EU advance or promote best interests as a principle, a right and a rule of procedure. The criminal justice results were published in June 2014 and the civil and administrative justice results in 2015.[157]

---

155. See Chapter 1.2.
156. See Chapter 1.1.
157. Kennan, N. and Kilkelly, U. (2015), Children's involvement in criminal, civil and administrative judicial proceedings in the 28 Member States of the EU. Policy brief, Publications Office of the European Union, Luxembourg. See also respective reports for each member state.

The majority of jurisdictions have reflected the principle that the best interests of the child should be a guiding force in decision making in their constitution (for example Belgium, Hungary, Slovenia and Spain) or in relevant legislation (for example Austria, Belgium, Bulgaria, Cyprus, Czech Republic, Denmark, Greece, France, Italy, Lithuania, Luxembourg, Malta, Slovenia, Slovakia, Spain, Sweden and the United Kingdom). However, in some jurisdictions (for example Belgium and Italy) the relevant legislation only refers to the need to take the child's best interests into account and does not state that the child's best interests should be a primary or paramount consideration. There is an essential difference between these two expressions.

In certain jurisdictions, specific references to the principle of advancing the child's best interests can only be found in civil judicial procedural codes and not administrative judicial procedural codes. The specific references may also be present in specific sectoral legislation concerning family disputes and child protection rather than other areas of law (such as in Malta). It would however be essential to consider best interests and their primacy in all cases, not only the most obvious ones.

In at least three member states (Cyprus, Estonia, Ireland) the principle is not enshrined in national legislation at all. In a handful of jurisdictions (such as Austria, Finland, the United Kingdom/ England, Wales and Scotland), criteria have been developed in legislation to help judges assess the best interests of the child in specific types of proceedings.

In some 11 member states (Belgium, Czech Republic, Denmark, Greece, Spain, Luxembourg, Latvia, the Netherlands, Poland, Slovenia, the United Kingdom/Northern Ireland), looser guidelines, or parameters, have been developed usually through the case law of higher courts, but also through legislation. In at least eight member states (Belgium, Croatia, Cyprus, Estonia, France, Lithuania, Portugal and Sweden) no such criteria or guidelines exist. In Sweden the absence of such criteria is deliberate as the government has reasoned that the authorities and courts need to have the flexibility and discretion to decide what is in the best interests of the child and to choose the most appropriate solution on a case-by-case basis.

Giving due weight to the expressed views of the child in civil and administrative proceedings is an essential component in considering his or her best interests in the manner required by Article 3 of the UNCRC. In several jurisdictions (for example, Bulgaria, Cyprus, Denmark, Greece, Finland, France, Italy, Lithuania, the Netherlands, Romania, Spain, Sweden, the United Kingdom), there is a legal obligation on the part of a court to hear the child and give due weight to his or her views before reaching a decision if he or she is considered mature enough. In Luxembourg, this measure is followed in practice even though there is no legal requirement for the child to be heard in order to assess his or her best interests.

In certain jurisdictions (such as Lithuania), this obligation only applies in the area of family law. Furthermore, in at least four jurisdictions (Ireland, Latvia, Portugal and Slovenia), the court is under no legal obligation to consider the views of the child in order to determine his or her best interests, although legislative changes are foreseen in Ireland in this regard (signed into law in April 2015).[158]

---

158. See http://www.dcya.gov.ie/viewdoc.asp?fn=/documents/Child_Welfare_Protection/ChildrensReferendum.htm.

Adopting a multidisciplinary approach can improve best-interests assessments. In civil and administrative proceedings in several member states (Austria, Bulgaria, Croatia, Denmark, Italy, Lithuania, Luxembourg, Malta, the Netherlands, Portugal, Romania, Slovenia, Spain), the court consults with professionals or experts from different disciplines in order to reach a holistic picture of the child's best interests. In some member states these consultations are not obligatory (for example, Italy or Luxembourg). In others, the consultations are only obligatory in family and placement into care proceedings (for example, Lithuania, Romania or Spain).

In general it can be stated that measures to ensure the effective implementation of the best interests of the child in judicial proceedings are more strongly developed in the areas of family and placement into care than in other areas of law. Some countries may not apply such measures to asylum and immigration law, for example. This is highly problematic, as the best interests of the child must be a primary consideration in all cases concerning children. If there is no best interests assessment can we be certain that the child's rights in general are respected?

In some jurisdictions, however, the principle that the best interests of the child should be a primary or paramount consideration is enshrined in specific sectoral laws pertaining to specific areas of administrative justice, such as asylum and migration (France, Greece, Italy, Slovenia, Sweden, Slovenia), health (France) and education (Sweden).

Given that the principle of the best interests of the child is enshrined in EU law, the European Commission will also be looking closely at how it can contribute to ensuring that the determination of the best interests is properly and objectively done to advance, as Nigel Cantwell states elsewhere in this publication,[159] the human rights of children.

---

159. See Chapter 1.2.

The concept of the best interests of the child from the perspective of a practitioner

Tam Baillie
Scotland's Commissioner for Children and Young People, Chairperson of the European Network of Ombudspersons for Children

I strongly believe in the principle of the best interests of the child as a primary consideration as required by the United Nations Convention on the Rights of the Child (UNCRC). In Scotland, we have the Children (Scotland) Act 1995, which requires that decisions made in respect of a child must have his or her welfare as the paramount consideration. However, best interests can be a challenging concept as there may be differing opinions as to what constitutes the best interests of the child. Even though welfare is an essential factor that has to be taken into account when assessing a child's best interests, the principle is much more multilayered and complex. In this text, I want to provide two perspectives regarding the application of the best interests of the child principle.

The first of these two perspectives is the application of best interests at a population level. This is most pertinent when considering economic, social and cultural rights – for instance Article 27 of the UNCRC, a child's right to an adequate standard of living – as opposed to civil and political rights. We know that children who do not have an adequate standard of living are more likely to experience a wide range of negative outcomes compared to those who live in affluent circumstances. Those without an adequate standard of living tend to live shorter lives, have poorer educational outcomes, suffer from mental health problems and have more difficulty entering the labour market.

In other words, many of the rights of children suffering from these problems are compromised as a result of living in poverty – and poverty affects millions of children in Europe. The issue is that economic policies should take account of children's best interests. However, the problem is that there is no meaningful redress when jurisdictions' economic policies do not take account of the impact on children. The result is children living in poverty, severely compromising their rights. Even though economic, social and cultural rights are as important as civil and political rights, the way they have been formulated in international conventions is often more open to interpretation and less absolute. Article 27 of the UNCRC, for instance, obliges states parties to take "appropriate measures" to assist parents.

My second perspective is the application of best interests for individual children. Here I want to give three practical examples which illustrate the challenges related to the application of the concept. First, we have an evolving understanding of the factors which need to be taken into account when children are taken into care. We have benefitted from the work of John Bowlby and others from the 1940s onwards, who highlighted the importance of attachment between baby and carer in the early years of life. Over the past 25 years this has been augmented by technological advances in magnetic resonance imaging (MRI) which measures brain development. The combined effect is that we can now measure the impact of different environmental influences on a baby's brain, thus identifying where poor parenting has a negative impact on a child's social, emotional and cognitive development. As a result, we are much better informed than previously as to the impact of different parenting styles on the development of our children.

This poses challenges for the application of best interests because many children live in circumstances where their development is not maximised through their family life, but not so compromised that they need to be removed from home. And if the child is removed from the family, it is not certain that state care will be any better – in some jurisdictions, including the Scottish one, the evidence is that children in care have poorer outcomes than those living at home.

We know that the bond with a main carer is a powerful protective factor for a child, so what is in the best interests of the child? Should children be left in circumstances which may not maximise their development, yet maintain their right to family life? Or, should the child be removed to an environment and carers who may (or may not) provide a more nurturing environment? The key challenge will be the application of judgment rather than the application of best interests, because it is not clear what constitutes best interests. What is considered to be in a child's best interests has changed over the years, being dependent on the available evidence, making it susceptible to contentious and inconsistent application.

The second example concerning the application of best interests for individual children is related to challenges in choosing suitable means for adequately implementing the best interests of the child in individual cases. In the 1980s, I set up and ran a unit for young people aged 16 to 21 who were homeless in Glasgow; we called it "Stopover". I know that the unit was a highly regarded one. You could tell this from the number of referrals that we received – we had an average of seven referrals for every bed. However, people were trying to get young people into Stopover, not just to relieve their homelessness, but because they knew they would have follow-on accommodation options.

Stopover had a reputation for listening to young people and paying attention to their views. We were in a very strong position, where professionals paid attention to our recommendations because we were assertive about what we thought were the young people's best interests. We could get them into housing, and in fact a large proportion of our young people moved on to independent accommodation. At that time, I was part of a lobby trying to get the right to housing for 16 and 17-year-olds and as a result many of our young people moved on to housing; some with a lot of support, some with a light touch, but we could move them on to independence.

I think we got it wrong. I think that despite my pride in managing Stopover and being able to set up the service on the basis of their best interests, we got it wrong. The reason I think we got it wrong is because our young people did not need a move to independence, and many could not cope with it so they became homeless again. What they needed was tender love and care. What they needed was a place where they could feel stable and wanted – not a move to independence. We were responding to their views on accommodation options and implementing these without applying our own judgment as to what was in their best interests. In fact, we should have paid much more attention to our own judgment and experience in what would actually be best for each young person concerned.

A third example of difficulties related to the application of the concept of best interests in individual cases is that we currently have a problem in Scotland responding to the best interests of children living in families where there is domestic abuse. This is especially so in instances where the victim of domestic abuse leaves the home and the perpetrator requests to have contact with the child. In many cases these disputes over child contact are resolved through court processes as the parents cannot agree what is in the child's best interests.

I am encouraged that the views of the child are frequently sought by the court as to what they wish to happen in terms of contact with the non-resident parent, who in the vast majority of cases is the father. The problem is that we know how traumatising an experience domestic abuse is and that children may have difficulty expressing their true feelings because of a range of factors. For instance, the child may feel that they are being disloyal to the father if they say they do not want to have contact. The child may equally want contact but is frightened of the abuser and needs to be assured they are protected during the contact. Then the child may not want contact but knows his or her younger siblings do and goes along with this.

There are also challenges in the way we seek children's views which may not be conducive to their sharing what they really feel. We do not necessarily know the views of the children involved, or we do not know how to interpret what they say. All of this makes decisions on contact arrangements difficult. Even in cases where the views of the child are known, the child may be expressing a wish for contact with a parent known to be violent but the judgment is that it would be better for the child not to have contact, creates a dilemma as to what is in the child's best interests.

In conclusion, I want to reiterate my strong support for the concept of best interests. The concept keeps the children at the centre of our concerns; we all know how easy it is to lose children in a swathe of other considerations when making decisions. The concept is ambitious in its scope because at a population level there are few, if any, means of redress to rectify wrongs when children's best interests are not honoured. At an individual level, having children's best interests as a focus is a worthy if challenging approach. That said, dealing with human beings is always a challenge. We need to apply best interests in all of our dealings with children – it is our responsibility to rise to the challenge this presents.

What is the input by children and young people in implementing their best interests?

Johanna Nyman
President of the European Youth Forum

The principle of the best interests of the child is one of the highlights of the United Nations Convention on the Rights of the Child (UNCRC). It may also be the most debated and studied principle of the convention. It is, without doubt, a principle that needs to be developed further in order to better interact with all the human rights safeguarded in the UNCRC. Today, we should put effort into ensuring that the convention as a whole is alive, effective, well known and used, as well as to making its principles understood, implemented and respected.

The four general principles of the UNCRC: non-discrimination, the best interests of the child as a primary consideration, right to life and development, and participation rights, are key when it comes to the protection and promotion of the rights of young people. These four principles should be applied together, and interpreted together, in order to achieve a holistic approach to children's rights.

From the perspective of child and youth organisations, participation is one of the most important aspects of the principle of the best interests of the child. Participation rights enshrined in Article 12 of the UNCRC are one of the unique features of the convention. Participation rights mean that children have the right to have a say in decisions affecting them. Their views should be listened to and given weight in decision making.

Participation is also one of the pillars of the work that the European Youth Forum conducts every day. The Youth Forum strives to increase the level and the equality of youth participation. This includes, for example, promoting the voting rights of youth, establishing youth structures, involving youth organisations and young people in decision making in an effective way as well as the implementation of co-management systems. The most effective way to encourage child and youth participation is through representative, democratic organisations. This is something that cannot be substituted, but could be complemented, by alternative and ad hoc forms of participation.

In its General Comment No. 14 on the right of the child to have his or her best interests taken as a primary consideration (Article 3.1), the United Nations Committee on the Rights of the Child acknowledged that listening to the child is an essential element of a successful best-interests assessment. In other words, the best interests of the child are not properly "considered" in a case affecting a child or children in the sense meant in Article 3.1 of the UNCRC if the child has not had a chance to express his or her views. This statement by the Committee gives participation an indispensable role from the point of view of best interests, since it means that the best interests of the child cannot be determined without listening to the child. We must move away from a traditional, paternalistic perception where adults create all the frames for the rights of the child and have the final say in determining what is in the best interests of the child.

The point is not, however, to have children decide everything by themselves. In child and youth participation the concept of evolving capacities is central. A child is not born with full capacities; these capacities develop little by little. The level of participation of a child always needs to be adapted to his or her current capacities. We cannot expect a child to participate in the same way as an adult, but this does not mean the child does not have opinions or that these opinions would not be valuable to the surrounding community. It is essential to listen to the child in order to make a good decision, a decision that can in fact be considered to grasp the nature of "best interests".

According to Article 1 of the UNCRC, the term child means every human being below the age of 18 unless according to the law applicable to the child, majority is attained earlier. At the moment almost everyone in the world agrees along the lines set by the UNCRC that anyone below 18 years old has the right to special care and protection.

At the same time, what happens just after one stops being a child according to the official age limit? As the UNCRC protects everyone under 18, young people aged 18 or older are excluded from its scope of application. One day there is the special protection and the next day the former child is expected to live an autonomous life without any positive discrimination. We see today that the transition from childhood to adulthood often takes longer than before. The transition also is more difficult for a huge number of young people. This transition needs to be investigated further, acknowledged and protected. There is a need to put in place more specific efforts towards the recognition and the protection of youth rights.

On the other hand, "one size fits all" solutions are not very effective due to some crucial differences in children and young people's status with regards to their needs and aspirations, their daily challenges and positions in society. For this reason, in-depth research on the status of young people's human rights as well as on the impact of policy measures on children and youth would be a good basis for further investigating the differences between traditional youth and children policies.

Young people above the age of 18 do not have a specific, powerful tool protecting their rights such as the UNCRC, with the exception of two regional charters: the African Youth Charter and the Ibero-American Convention on the Rights of Youth. Despite these two instruments specialised in protecting youth rights, young people do not necessarily enjoy their rights in the way they should. Different institutions and non-governmental organisations have highlighted in various ways the serious barriers that youth face today in accessing their rights. They have also highlighted how the lack of a specific tool, as well as the recent economic and financial crisis, has worsened the situation.

From a youth perspective, the principle of the best interests of the child is still very clear and necessary. Too often we see laws, actions, policies and measures affecting young people in their daily lives that do not put their best interests first and can thus have serious and damaging effects. The extreme labour market liberalisation and fragmentation and the promotion of more and more precarious jobs for youth also have a detrimental effect on young people's possibilities in life – and weaken their possibilities to access their rights.

One of the ways to ensure the respect of the principle of the best interests of the child is to make sure children and young people participate in society. A chance to actively participate means not only that children and young people are heard in specific cases regarding their well-being, but that there is a constant involvement of children and young people in designing policies and measures that respect the principle of participation.

The Optional Protocol to the Convention on the Rights of the Child on a communications procedure, which came into force on 14 April 2014 after 10 states had ratified it, has opened up new possibilities for children under the age of 18 to participate in decisions affecting them. These possibilities make it more accessible and easier to directly challenge and lodge complaints of children's rights violations. The system of individual complaints could play a crucial role in making the UNCRC more respected and well known, as well as in increasing children and youth's ownership and awareness of their rights. Youth and children's rights organisations should focus on specific advocacy activities to target states and ask them to ratify this Optional Protocol.

Nowadays, more than ever, it is crucial and urgent to work on the empowerment of children and youth as active citizen s in a complex society. This also contributes towards their full well-being. Participatory research is needed to get a clearer picture of the challenges children and young people face today. More effective policy measures should be jointly designed and co-evaluated by decision makers, children and young people. I would like to quote an important saying from friends working in the disability field: "Nothing for us without us!"

Ethical pointers and framework for taking decisions in a child's best interests – The perspective of a children's ombudsman

Bernard De Vos
Former President of the European Network of Ombudspersons for Children (ENOC), General Delegate for children's rights of the Wallonia-Brussels Federation, Belgium

A question of meaning and a question of ethics: How can it be decided whether a given act, a given judgment, is good or bad? What is best for a child at a given time and in a given society? What is the best solution for that child today that will remain so tomorrow?

The question of a child's best interests is closely linked with a culture, with bodies of knowledge, with a concept of the person, the child and the family. If ethical pointers are to be given, it should first be emphasised that the notion of the best interests of the child entails two realities and two specific assessments. The first is an abstract, general assessment which is valid for all children. For example, it is widely held that children should not be ill-treated and should live in a family setting.

The second is a tangible assessment of a very precise situation where, besides considering the different rights enshrined in the United Nations Convention on the Rights of the Child (UNCRC), which are unfortunately sometimes contradictory, the interests of a given child must be considered. To take the same example, should a particular child who is subjected to ill-treatment within his/her family be separated from the family or not? These are therefore two different assessments and, since the second has been much discussed, I should like to enter into a little more detail regarding the more abstract and general assessment.

The principle of the child's best interests, implying that children should be a priority in our society, would certainly gain by being better known. If, more than 25 years after its adoption, we must note with regret that the Convention on the Rights of the Child is still too little known and still too often infrequently applied, that is perhaps in the end due to the inadequacy of our awareness-raising efforts. Perhaps too, we have involuntarily robbed the convention of its power by limiting its discussion to closed fora, conferences, colloquies and symposia.

I nevertheless think that we could make the best interests of the child a popular concern, ensuring that this requirement to prioritise children filters down and genuinely pervades our day-to-day realities at school, in the family or in other areas such as mobility, urban ecology and citizen participation. I firmly believe that the rights of the child and the child's best interests are issues which should be raised on a far broader level and not be confined to a restricted circle of specialists gathered together in colloquies.

UNICEF has reported that 2014 was a devastating year for children: from Syria to Nigeria, from Afghanistan to Gaza, no fewer than 15 million children were caught in the trap of ever deadlier and heavier fighting. These millions of children killed, executed or exiled are the first victims of our modern battlefields. And one need not look far to become outraged: today in Brussels, a provincial town on a worldwide scale but called "the capital of Europe", a small town which extols its interculturalism as a tourist attraction – a very high level of discrimination exists and incredible poverty is experienced on an ever larger scale. There are dozens of children sleeping in the open, living in filthy squats, exposed to vermin and insecurity, on the simple pretext that their parents are without the proper administrative documents.

I think societal changes cannot be triggered in confined surroundings at the behest of experts, however competent they may be. They come about through shifts in the balance of powers, and it behoves us to instigate such transitions, without delay, for the benefit of children. While we must continue meeting among ourselves and, as has been said, training professionals in the best possible way, we must also reach out and raise awareness in the locations where people are to be found, where they live, in the marketplaces, in amusement parks, in leisure parks. It is necessary to be present where people live in order to ensure that children's best interests are maximised whenever necessary.

Maximising children's best interests also entails combating their manipulation. It has been pointed out on several occasions that the UNCRC can be made to say anything and everything, and Article 3 likewise. This was the case in France with the wide-ranging movement opposed to marriage for all: initially the objectors contended that the convention recommended that every child should have a father and a mother whereas, if the convention is re-read attentively, that is quite untrue. Next, they fell back on the child's best interests.

Another older example concerns the principle of custody or alternating residence, which has certainly suited a lot of children and has always been presented as a measure meant to be in the child's best interests. It is surely reasonable to think that alternating residence had the primary aim of considerably reducing the number of cases brought before the courts and lessening the impact of family separations on the cost of justice.

I therefore recommend that we collectively keep alert and ensure that the convention and the concept of the child's interests are directly disseminated within society, and that we remain watchful in order to position ourselves clearly and refuse any form of manipulation.

To conclude as regards the concrete assessment of a precise situation, I would quote Pierre Verbier, a French lawyer, who works directly with young people: "Claiming to know the child's interests is a colonialist attitude." He also added that it was often the ideological leanings of a judge, a head teacher or a placement official which determined the child's supposed interests. The child's interests are seldom expressed by the child, but are decided by others and ultimately, as Nigel Cantwell suggests, they can become inimical to the rights of the child.[160]

Another fundamental ethical concern is enabling children to speak out. It must be a constant aim to allow them to be heard on all subjects concerning children, and also on subjects that do not directly concern them. We would certainly derive benefits from being receptive to the spontaneous, uncensored views of children on a whole series of questions confronting our society: ecology and eco-citizenship, mobility in urban areas, provision for the elderly, etc. They plainly have an original outlook on these questions which would be enriching for us and could work towards the collective interests.

Finally, I wish to speak of one of my memories of my period in office as children's rights defender in French-speaking Belgium, which particularly marked me as regards these ethical pointers. It concerns the night before my senate hearing on the subject of euthanasia of children. Over 10 years ago, Belgium enacted legislation enabling certain adults under certain conditions to ask to receive euthanasia. More recently the senate looked into the possibility of making this option available to children.

I admit that I had a difficult night because the next day I would be obliged to say quite weighty things which could have serious repercussions. In this debate, what mattered was not so much the extension or otherwise of euthanasia to minors, but rather the conditions under which it was to be implemented. The question had more bearing on whether to introduce a minimum age – 12 years old for example – and of course have legal certainty, which is important, or whether to put the child's best interests first and consider that certain children, with their experience of life, attain a far earlier maturity and discernment than other children, in particular circumstances. From an ethical perspective, this is a situation which raises many questions.

To conclude, I would briefly mention the issue of families. Since the adoption of the UNCRC, families have changed in an astounding manner. From conventional families – father, mother, two children – we have now progressed to homoparental, single-parent, multi-parent and reconstituted families. All these patterns exist today. Even the manner of conceiving children has evolved; it is still possible to have children in the old-fashioned way, but one can also deep-freeze genetic material,

---

160. See Chapter 1.2.

travel to India or Ukraine and come back with a child who will be physically in good condition but whose filiation will be far from guaranteed.

These are very important questions, and alas they are not entirely settled by the various articles of the convention. However, the concept of the child's best interests allows discussion-based reflection, which provides the legislator with tools for intervening and clarifying the situation of children who are sometimes subject to terrible legal uncertainty. We might in particular bear in mind the many children who are recognised under the *kafala* (Muslim sponsorship) system but refused for adoption, those born of surrogate mothers and deprived of the legal filiation to which they are nevertheless entitled.

Great care must be taken concerning children's best interests in relation to these new questions of ethics and bioethics in certain individual situations which are constantly being brought to our attention in our independent institutions for the defence of children's rights.

The best interests of the child and current challenges civil society faces

Jana Hainsworth
Eurochild Secretary General

Eurochild is a European umbrella network representing over 170 organisations and individuals who are working with and for children and young people across Europe. Many of our members are themselves networks or international organisations. We are primarily concerned with advocacy and influence towards the European Union and using EU leverage to support better policies and investment at national level. The work of Eurochild is based on the values of the United Nations Convention on the Rights of the Child (UNCRC), including the principle of the best interests of the child.

Civil society is by nature very diverse and represents different views. Its added value is to bring different opinions into discussion. This text discusses the best interests of the child in the context of different practical problems civil society faces today. How could civil society participate in achieving a greater understanding of the best interests of the child? What are the most important challenges we need to overcome to be able to continue our work in an efficient way and truly act "in the best interests of the child"?

As a representative of civil society, I feel a certain sense of responsibility when speaking about the best interests of the child. The best interests of the child are a difficult and ambitious topic, a complex concept in general. This concept is also central to the work of all the professionals working with children or with questions related to children including in civil society. The best interests of the child can serve as a helpful tool for civil society in its efforts to protect children's rights. On the other hand, it can have damaging effects if misused, as Nigel Cantwell suggests in his text.

The concept of the best interests of the child has different dimensions. According to the United Nations Committee on the Rights on the Child, it is a substantive right, a procedural rule and a guiding principle. While acknowledging concerns raised by legal experts related to the nature of the concept, I want to underline that the concept of the best interests of the child can and should be used to mainstream the rights of the child in practical work. It should be used to make sure children's rights are taken into account in policy areas where they might not otherwise be considered. We need to put the rights and well-being of children at the very heart of the policy debate and mainstream a child-rights approach across all professional sectors coming into daily contact with children.

In this regard, a rights-based understanding of the principle of the best interests of the child is essential. The best interests of the child are not just any interests, since the concept is connected to the human rights of children in an inalienable way. When the relevant human rights are respected, the best interests of the child are considered in the sense of Article 3.1 of the UNCRC. As the Committee on the Rights of the Child recalls in its General Comment No. 14 on the right of the child to have his or her best interests taken as a primary consideration, there is no hierarchy of rights in the UNCRC; all the rights provided for are in the "child's best interests", and no right could be compromised by a negative interpretation of the child's best interests.[161]

The concept of the best interests of the child has theoretical dimensions, but it also has a very central role in our practical work. Recently there has been many positive developments at policy level; children's rights are nowadays getting a lot more attention than before. At Eurochild, we are encouraged by the growing attention and political importance accorded to children's rights both by the European Union and the Council of Europe. The European Parliament Resolution on the 25th Anniversary of the UNCRC was adopted at the end of 2014. The resolution was an important landmark. It underlines the importance of addressing the issue of children's rights in the agenda of the European Union as well as the importance of considering children as a priority in future regional and cohesion policies. The resolution explicitly states that the rights of the child, including the principle of the best interests of the child, concern all EU policies, not only those directed at children. It equally

> calls on the Member States to ensure that the principle of the best interests of the child is respected in all legislation, in decisions taken by government representatives at all levels and in all court decisions, and encourages the Member States to share best practices with a view to improving the correct application of the principle of the best interests of the child across the EU.[162]

We are also happy that a specific Intergroup on Children's Rights was recently established dedicated to mainstreaming children's rights throughout EU policy, especially in the European Parliament. One of the aims of the intergroup is to ensure that the best interests of the child are taken into account.

In addition, the adoption of the European Commission's Recommendation "Investing in children: breaking the cycle of disadvantage" in 2013 captured much of what we as civil society have been saying for some time about the necessity for a holistic and child-rights approach to tackling child poverty and promoting children's well-being. The recommendation underlines the importance of establishing policies that take children's rights and well-being into account in advance. It is remarkable proof of the

---

161. UN Committee on the Rights of the Child, General Comment No. 14 (2013) on the right of the child to have his or her best interests taken as a primary consideration (Article 3.1), paragraph 4.
162. European Parliament resolution on the 25th anniversary of the UN Convention on the Rights of the Child (2014/2919(RSP)).

significant role children play in each society. The recommendation on investing in children clearly states that investment in prevention and early intervention is crucial. It is less costly and more effective to intervene when problems are quite small and quite new. Once problems have escalated and become more complex they are much more difficult and more costly to resolve. Unfortunately, while this principle might be understood in theory, in practice budget cuts hit prevention hardest.

The Council of Europe has conducted a rights-based children's programme "Building a Europe for and with children" since 2006. The programme was set up to secure and promote children's human rights, and to protect children from violence. Different guidelines adopted by the Council of Europe have been useful for the work of Eurochild, including the guidelines on child-friendly justice. The Council of Europe Committee of Ministers has also adopted important recommendations, for instance on child participation, child and family-friendly social services, positive parenting and violence prevention.[163]

Even though this important work by the European Union, the Council of Europe and others exists and flourishes, we also need a reality check. Across Europe levels of child poverty and social exclusion are escalating. Eurochild members are working on a daily basis with some of the most vulnerable children and young people. While the demand for our work is growing, many organisations face resource constraints and budget cuts. Some services have to close due to a lack of funding. In addition to the economic crisis, the current refugee crisis is another challenge that contributes to rising levels of child poverty.

Child poverty is one of the biggest challenges in the work of civil society, since it is an important barrier to children's access to their rights. Therefore it also has a connection to the best interests of the child, as the best interests of the child require that children's rights are fully taken into account. Addressing child poverty is crucial for society as a whole, not only for the individual. The "Austerity Bites" exhibition, developed as a collaboration between the European Network of Ombudspersons for Children and the Council of Europe, gives a unique insight into how children and young people are experiencing the effects of the crisis and the government driven austerity measures that followed.

I am missing a real sense of urgency in acting in the best interests of children. We all share a responsibility to make real improvements in the lives of children. I urge government representatives to act to influence policy, practice and spending and promote children's rights more broadly. Without support from public authorities, civil society cannot work in an efficient way.

---

163. Recommendation CM/Rec(2012)2 of the Committee of Ministers to member States on the participation of children and young people under the age of 18; Recommendation CM/Rec(2011)12 of the Committee of Ministers to member states on children's rights and social services friendly to children and families; Recommendation Rec(2006)19 of the Committee of Ministers to member states on policy to support positive parenting; Recommendation CM/Rec(2009)10 of the Committee of Ministers to member states on integrated national strategies for the protection of children from violence.

Chapter 4

Best interests of the
child in family affairs

Jurisprudence of the European Court of Human Rights on the best interests of the child in family affairs

Aida Grgić
Lawyer, European Court of Human Rights[164]

The European Convention on Human Rights (the Convention) is an international instrument guaranteeing basic civil and political rights to all persons, including children, falling within the jurisdiction of one of its signatory states. However, it is not a specialised children's rights convention. The Convention explicitly mentions children in several of its provisions, notably in Articles 5[165] and 6.[166] It also guarantees the right to education, which for the most part – though not exclusively – relates to children. The Convention provisions which have been shown to have particular relevance to children in the jurisprudence of the European Court of Human Rights (the Court) are Article 8, which guarantees the right to respect for private and family life and Article 3, which in absolute terms prohibits torture, inhuman and degrading treatment and punishment.

Unlike the United Nations Convention on the Rights of the Child (UNCRC), the Convention does not expressly refer to "the best interests of the child". However, the European Court of Human Rights has developed a large body of case law dealing with children's rights and has on numerous occasions dealt with the best interests concept in various contexts, such as juvenile justice and migrant children.

---

164. Views expressed in this paper are the author's personal opinions and they do not in any way bind the Registry or the Court.
165. Article 5.1. *d* provides for lawful detention of minors for the purposes of educational supervision or bringing them before the competent legal authority.
166. Article 6.1 allows the exclusion of public from a trial where the interests of juveniles so require.

This article will concentrate exclusively on family matters and thus on Article 8 of the Convention. That said, it is crucial to understand that the European Court of Human Rights operates as an application-driven system. Guided by the principle of subsidiarity, it leaves the assessment of relevant facts primarily to the national authorities and intervenes only when the decision of those authorities do not appear to be Convention compliant. Finally, the Court does not operate in a vacuum and it draws inspiration from other binding international legal instruments. In addition to being attentive to standard setting and other activities within the Council of Europe, in the application of the Convention in children's rights cases the Court is particularly mindful of specialised children's rights instruments such as the UNCRC and the Hague Convention on the Civil Aspects of International Child Abduction.

Custody and access rights

The first large group of family cases which allowed the Court to develop its jurisprudence related to children, and thereby draw on the best interests concept, concerns the area of custody and access rights. The Court has frequently stated that mutual enjoyment by parent and child of each other's company constituted a fundamental element of family life even when the relationship between the parents had broken down.[167] Domestic measures hindering enjoyment of family life – such as a decision granting custody of children to one parent – constitute an interference with the right to respect for family life, which will result in a violation of Article 8 of the Convention unless it is "in accordance with the law", pursues a legitimate aim and can be regarded as "necessary in a democratic society".

In applying this "necessity" test, the Court has to consider whether, in the light of the case as a whole, the reasons adduced by the domestic courts to justify this measure were relevant and sufficient for the purposes of Article 8 of the Convention. In this context, it must be borne in mind that the national authorities have the benefit of direct contact with all the persons concerned. The Court's task is thus not to substitute itself for the domestic authorities in the exercise of their responsibilities regarding custody and access issues, but rather to review, in the light of the Convention, the decisions taken by those authorities in the exercise of their power of appreciation.[168] The "margin of appreciation" accorded to the competent national authorities will vary according to the nature of the issue and the importance of the interests at stake. The margin of appreciation can be rather wide when deciding on custody matters, but narrower as regards any further limitations on parental rights of access since those entail the danger that the family relations between the parents and a young child might be effectively curtailed.[169]

In sum, Article 8 requires that the domestic authorities strike a fair balance between the interests of the child and those of the parents and that, in the balancing process, particular importance is attached to the best interests of the child, which, depending

---

167. See, for example, *Diamante and Pelliccioni v. San Marino*, No. 32250/08, paragraph 170, 27 September 2011.
168. See *Hokkanen v. Finland*, 19823/92, 23 September 1994, paragraph 55, Series A No. 299A.
169. See *T.P. and K.M. v. the United Kingdom* [GC], No. 28945/95, paragraph 71, ECHR 2001V (extracts).

on their nature and seriousness, may override those of the parents.[170] In particular, a parent cannot be entitled under Article 8 to have such measures taken as would harm the child's health and development.

Finally, the Court has developed a procedural requirement that the entire decision-making process concerning respect for family life must be fair and afford due respect to the interests protected by Article 8. What must be considered is whether the parents have been involved in the decision-making process to a degree sufficient to provide them with a requisite protection of their interests, including keeping them informed about developments, ensuring that they can participate in decisions made about them,[171] and in certain circumstances hearing from the children concerned.[172]

It is precisely this last issue – the necessity of hearing the child in court – that was at the heart of *Sahin v. Germany*.[173] In that case the applicant was denied access to his daughter because it was concluded that their contacts would be harmful to the child due to the serious tensions between the parents. On the question of hearing the child in court, the Court recalled that, as a general rule it was for the national courts to assess the evidence before them, including the means used to ascertain the relevant facts.[174] It would be going too far under Article 8 of the Convention to say that domestic courts were always required to hear a child in court on the issue of access rights to a parent who does not have custody. This issue had to be assessed in light of specific circumstances of each case, having due regard to the age and maturity of the child concerned. In the *Sahin* case the Court referred to the explanation provided by the domestic expert who, after several meetings with the child, her mother and the applicant, plausibly explained that the very process of questioning the child entailed a risk for her well-being, which could not be avoided by special arrangements in court. In such circumstances direct questioning of the child had not been in her best interests.

In another access case, *P.V. v. Spain*,[175] a male-to-female transsexual complained about the restrictions on access to her son on account of her gender reassignment. The national courts emphasised that the applicant's transsexualism was not the reason for restricting the contacts, but instead that the child's best interests required such a measure, which would allow the child to become gradually accustomed to his father's new identity. The national courts had taken into account the applicant's emotional instability attested by a psychological expert report and the risk that it might negatively affect the mental well-being and the development of personality of her six-year-old child. In addition, new contact arrangements were made on a gradual and reviewable basis, as recommended in the expert report. Consequently the Court found no violation of Article 8 in conjunction with Article 14 of the Convention.

---

170. See *Görgülü v. Germany*, No. 74969/01, paragraph 43, 26 February 2004; *Sommerfeld v. Germany* [GC], No. 31871/96, paragraph 64, ECHR 2003VIII (extracts).

171. See W. v. the United Kingdom, No. 9749/82, 8 July 1987; McMichael v. the United Kingdom, No. 16424/90, 24 February 1995.

172. See B. v. Romania (No. 2) No. 1285/03, 19 February 2013; B.B. and F.B. v. Germany, Nos. 18734/09 and 9424/11, 14 March 2013.

173. *Sahin v. Germany* [GC], No. 30943/96, ECHR 2003VIII.

174. See *Vidal v. Belgium*, 12351/86, 22 April 1992, paragraph 33, Series A No. 235B.

175. *P.V. v. Spain*, no. 35159/09, 30 November 2010.

Another good example in the context of access rights would be the case of *Anayo v. Germany,*[176] which concerned the refusal of the German courts to grant the applicant, the biological but not the legal father of twins, access to his children. The domestic courts failed to give any consideration to the question whether such contact, in the circumstances, would have been in the children's best interests, thereby violating Article 8. Consequently, Article 8 could be interpreted as imposing an obligation on states to examine whether it was in the child's best interests to allow the biological father to establish a relationship with his child, for example by granting him contact rights. However, this does not necessarily imply a duty under the Convention to allow the biological father to challenge paternity of the legal father.[177]

As regards the situation where children are otherwise separated from their parent, for example as a result of the parent's imprisonment, in *Horych v. Poland*[178] the Court has specifically addressed the issue of conditions in which the applicant, categorised as a dangerous prisoner, had received visits from his minor daughters. It noted that:

> visits from children ... in prison required special arrangements and may be subjected to specific conditions depending on their age, possible effects on their emotional state or well-being and on the personal circumstances of the person visited.

The Court went on to say that:

> positive obligations of the State under Article 8, included a duty to secure the appropriate, as stress-free for visitors as possible, conditions for receiving visits from his children, regard being had to the practical consequences of imprisonment.

Identity issues: paternity, maternity and surrogacy

In addition to custody and access rights, another area in which the Court has regularly examined the best interests of the child pertains to filiation – either maternal or paternal – and, more generally, to identity issues. Typically, claims before the Court are brought either by putative fathers unable to lodge a paternity claim, or by children prevented from filing, or unsuccessful in, a paternity claim against their presumed father.

When deciding whether Article 8 has been complied with in either of those situations, the Court seeks to determine whether, on the facts of the case, a fair balance has been struck by the state between the competing rights and interests at stake. In this context, the Court frequently recalled that the expression "everyone" in Article 8 of the Convention applies to both the child and the putative father. On the one hand, people have a right to know their origins, that right being derived from a wide interpretation of the scope of the notion of private life.[179] A person has a vital interest, protected by the Convention, in receiving information necessary to uncover the truth about an important aspect of his or her personal identity and eliminate

---

176. *Anayo v. Germany*, No. 20578/07, 21 December 2010.
177. See *Chavdarov v. Bulgaria*, No. 3465/03, 21 December 2010; and *Ahrens v. Germany*, No. 45071/09, 22 March 2012.
178. *Horych v. Poland*, No. 13621/08, paragraph 131, 17 April 2012.
179. See *Odièvre v. France* [GC], No. 42326/98, paragraph 29, ECHR 2003III.

any uncertainty in this respect.[180] On the other hand, a putative father's interest in being protected from claims concerning facts that go back many years cannot be denied. Finally, in addition to that conflict of interest, other interests may come into play, such as those of third parties, for example the putative father's family, and the general interest of legal certainty. The following examples are good illustrations of the Court's approach in these types of situations and clearly set out the child's best interests in the particular circumstances of each case.

In *Krisztián Barnabás Tóth v. Hungary*,[181] after carrying out a careful weighing of the child's best interests, the domestic authorities refused to bring a paternity action on behalf of the applicant, whose child born out of wedlock had already been recognised by another man and adopted by his wife. The Custody Board's home visit conducted with the adoptive family concluded that the child had developed emotional ties with, and was integrated into, a family which provided her with the necessary care and support. Establishment of the applicant's paternity would deprive the child of her existing loving family and social environment, potentially causing such damage to her that this could not be outweighed by the putative father's interest in having a biological fact established. In those circumstances, the Court was satisfied that the domestic authorities carried out a thorough scrutiny of the interests of those involved – attaching particular weight to the best interests of the child while not ignoring those of the applicant – and that there had been no violation of Article 8.

The Court reached a similar conclusion in *Chavdarov v. Bulgaria*,[182] where a biological father living with his three children was unable to contest the paternity of the mother's husband. The Court noted that the existence of the family formed by the applicant and his three children had never been threatened by the authorities, by the mother or by her husband and that, in the absence of a European-wide consensus on whether domestic legislation should enable the biological father to contest the presumption of a husband's paternity, the states enjoyed a wide margin of appreciation in regulating paternal filiation.

In *A.M.M. v. Romania*[183] the applicant's mother brought unsuccessful paternity proceedings, in which the putative father never reported to court-ordered forensic medical testing or attended court hearings. The Court observed that the guardianship office, which had been responsible under domestic law for protecting the interests of minors, never took part in the proceedings nor did the authorities apply any other measures to protect the child's interests, even though both the child and the mother were severely disabled. There had consequently been a violation of Article 8.

Finally, in *Krušković v. Croatia*[184] the Court found a violation of Article 8 of the Convention in respect of a man who was unable to be registered as the father of his biological child born out of wedlock, because he had been deprived of legal capacity. The Court reiterated that children "born out of wedlock also had a vital interest in

---

180. See *Mikulić v. Croatia*, No. 53176/99, paragraph 64, ECHR 2002-I.
181. *Krisztián Barnabás Tóth v. Hungary*, No. 48494/06, 12 February 2013.
182. *Chavdarov v. Bulgaria*, No. 3465/03, 21 December 2010.
183. *A.M.M. v. Romania*, No. 2151/10, 14 February 2012.
184. *Krušković v. Croatia*, No. 46185/08, paragraph 41, 21 June 2011.

receiving information necessary to uncover the truth about an important aspect of their personal identity, that is, the identity of their biological parents".

Fewer cases were examined as regards the establishment of maternity. Following the Grand Chamber finding of no violation of Article 8 in *Odievre v. France*[185] given that the French Government had meanwhile amended domestic legislation, in *Godelli v. Italy*[186] the applicant, who had been abandoned at birth, was unable to access information concerning her origins. Where the birth mother had opted not to disclose her identity, the Italian legislation did not provide any means for a child who was adopted and had not been formally recognised at birth to request access to non-identifying information on his or her origins or the waiver of confidentiality by the mother. The Court considered that the Italian authorities had overstepped their margin of appreciation.

The above-explained case law concerning identity has recently been applied in the context of novel medically assisted procreation techniques. This was another opportunity for the Court to underline the best interests of the child approach it has consistently taken in children's rights cases.

In *Mennesson v. France*[187] the applicants became parents of twins using surrogacy treatment in the United States. Following their return to France, they were unable to enter the children's birth certificates into the French register of birth on public-policy grounds. The Court accepted that the lack of recognition in French law of the parent-child relationship between the applicants affected their family life on various levels, but it did not find that the practical difficulties they faced had been insurmountable or that the applicants were prevented from exercising their right to respect for family life. They were able to settle in France shortly after the birth of the children, to live there together in circumstances which, by and large, were comparable to those of other families, and there was nothing to suggest that they were at risk of being separated by the authorities because of their situation in the eyes of French law. Given that there was no European consensus in this area and the consequent state's wide margin of appreciation, the Court found no violation of the "family life" aspect of the applicants' complaint.

In examining the "private life" complaint of the applicant children, the Court accepted that France might well wish to discourage its nationals from having recourse abroad to a reproductive technique prohibited inside the country. However, the effects of the refusal to recognise a parent-child relationship in French law between children conceived in this way and the intended parents were not confined to the situation of only the parents, who chose the disputed reproductive technique. The effects also extended to the situation of children themselves, whose right to respect for their private life – which implied that everyone should be able to establish the essence of his or her identity, including his or her parentage – was significantly affected. There was therefore a serious issue as to the compatibility of that situation with the children's best interests, which must guide any decision concerning them. In the applicants'

---

185. *Odièvre v. France* [GC], No. 42326/98, ECHR 2003III.
186. *Godelli v. Italy*, No. 33783/09, 25 September 2012.
187. Mennesson v. France, No. 65192/11, ECHR 2014 (extracts); see also Labassee v. France, No. 65941/11, 26 June 2014.

case, one of the intended parents was also the children's biological father. Given the importance of biological parentage as a component of each individual's identity, it could not be said that it was in the children's best interests to deprive them of a legal tie of this nature when both the biological reality of that tie was established and the children and the parent concerned sought its full recognition. Given the implications of this serious restriction in terms of the identity of the applicant children and their right to respect for private life, as well as the importance attached to the child's best interests, the Court held that France had overstepped its permissible margin of appreciation.

Placement in care

The Court has further examined the best interests of the child in cases concerning placement into care. In that context the Court has stressed that, following removal into care, any further limitations by the authorities entailed the danger that the family relations between the parents and a young child might be effectively curtailed.[188]

In its case law[189] the Court explained that the child's best interests comprised two parts. On the one hand, the interests clearly entailed ensuring that the child developed in a sound environment. On the other hand, it was equally in the child's best interests to maintain ties with his or her biological family, except in cases where the family proved particularly unfit. It followed that the interests of the child dictated that family ties may only be severed in very exceptional circumstances and that everything must be done to preserve personal relations and, if and when appropriate, to "rebuild" the family.[190] In the interest not only of the parent concerned, but also of the child, the ultimate aim of any "care order" must be to "reunite the ... parent with his or her child".[191]

In *Wallová and Walla v. the Czech Republic*[192] the applicants complained about the placement of their five children in alternative care due to their inadequate housing and financial situation. The Court found that instead of advising the family on how to improve their housing situation by way of applying for state aid or social housing, the authorities opted for the drastic measure of taking their children away from them. Interestingly, in its judgment the Court cited final observations of the UN Committee on the Rights of the Child which criticised the Czech legislation and policies affecting children and observed the increasing number of children placed in institutions by preliminary injunction. The Court concluded to a breach of Article 8.[193]

In *Levin v. Sweden*[194] the applicant complained about insufficient contact with her three children placed in public care. However, from the very negative physical

---

188. See *Johansen v. Norway*, 17383/90, 7 August 1996, paragraph 64, *Reports of Judgments and Decisions* 1996III; *Kutzner v. Germany*, No. 46544/99, paragraph 67, ECHR 2002I.
189. See *Gnahoré v. France*, No. 40031/98, paragraph 59, ECHR 2000IX.
190. Ibid.
191. See *Olsson v. Sweden (no. 1)*, 10465/83, 24 March 1988, paragraph 81, Series A No. 130; and *E.P. v. Italy*, No. 31127/96, paragraph 64, 16 November 1999.
192. *Wallová and Walla v. the Czech Republic*, No. 23848/04, 26 October 2006.
193. See also *R.M.S. v. Spain*, No. 28775/12, 18 June 2013.
194. *Levin v. Sweden*, No. 35141/06, 15 March 2012.

and mental reactions of the children before, during and after meetings with the applicant – notably their anxiety, bed wetting, nightmares and the regression in their development – the domestic courts found that the applicant's contact rights had to be limited in order to protect the children from further harm to their development and health and to ensure that they would have some stability and calm in their daily lives. This was also found to be necessary so that the children could begin to evolve in those areas where they were lacking and to develop positively without the regular set-backs that the meetings with their mother caused. Given that their father also sought contact rights, in order not to cause too much anxiety for the children, the social services had to balance the interest of each parent to see their children against the children's continued positive development, resulting in fewer visits for each parent, which the Court found to be a logical solution to ensure that the best interests of the children were protected. All of the foregoing enabled the Court to conclude that there had been no violation of Article 8 of the Convention.

Finally, in *B.B. and F.B. v. Germany*,[195] following allegations from the applicants' 12-year-old daughter that she and her younger brother had been repeatedly beaten by their father, the domestic court transferred parental authority from the applicants and placed the children in a care home. About a year later, the daughter admitted that she had lied about having been beaten and the children were eventually returned to their parents. Although mistaken assessments by professionals did not necessarily mean that measures taken would be incompatible with Article 8, the Court attached weight to the fact that the District Court relied only on the statements of the children, ignoring proof from medical professionals submitted by the applicants stating the opposite. As the children were in a safe placement at the time of the custody hearing, there had been no need for haste and the courts could have further investigated the facts of their own motion, which they failed to do. Consequently, the Court concluded that the German authorities had failed to give sufficient reasons for their decision to withdraw parental authority from the applicants and that there had therefore been a violation of Article 8.

Adoption

In cases concerning placement of a child for adoption, which entails a permanent severance of family ties, the best interests of the child need to be paramount instead of primary. As already stated, family ties may only be severed in very exceptional circumstances and it is not enough to show that a child could be placed in a more beneficial environment for his or her upbringing.[196] However, where the maintenance of family ties would harm the child's health and development, a parent is not entitled under Article 8 to insist that such ties be maintained. The Court's approach to these matters is best illustrated by the following examples.

In *Aune v. Norway*[197] the applicant's son had been placed into foster care when he was five months old after serious domestic abuse by his then drug-addict parents. The

---

195. *B.B. and F.B. v. Germany*, Nos. 18734/09 and 9424/11, 14 March 2013.
196. See *K. and T. v. Finland* [GC], No. 25702/94, paragraph 173, ECHR 2001-VII; *T.S. and D.S. v. the United Kingdom* (dec.), No. 61540/09, 19 January 2010.
197. *Aune v. Norway*, No. 52502/07, 28 October 2010.

child was eventually freed for adoption by his foster parents, the domestic authorities having established that, despite an improvement in the applicant's situation, she had still been unable to care for her son. The child had no emotional or social attachment to his biological mother, but instead remained vulnerable and needed reassurance that he would stay with his foster parents. Given the overall circumstances of the case – including a potential family conflict concerning the child's placement into foster care – the Court found that the domestic authorities had given relevant and sufficient reason as to why it had been in the child's best interests to replace the foster-care arrangement with a more far-reaching type of measure, namely depriving the applicant of parental responsibilities and authorisation of adoption. There had thus been no violation of Article 8.

In *Ageyevy v. Russia*[198] the applicants' adoption of two children was revoked by the domestic courts after one of them was injured in what the applicant claimed to have been an accident. The Court accepted that in the circumstances the suspicion of child abuse on the part of the parents could have justified the temporary removal of the children from them and thus found no violation of Article 8 in respect of that decision. Certain further contact restrictions between the applicants and the children pending a more detailed criminal investigation into the matter could also have been accepted. However, such a suspicion alone, in the absence of other weighty reasons, could not be sufficient for the revocation of the applicants' adoption. The relevant domestic decisions took no account of any damage to the emotional security and psychological condition of each child that might result from the sudden breaking of existing bonds with their adoptive parents, regard being had, in particular, to the children's age at the time. In other words the court decisions revoking the adoption had not been sufficiently justified, which led the Court to find a breach of Article 8 on this account.

In *Harroudj v. France*[199] the applicant had been allowed to take an Algerian girl into legal care (*kafala*), but not to adopt her because the family law of the child's country of origin made no provision for adoption. Even though *kafala* was not equal to adoption, it produced comparable effects to legal guardianship or placement with a view to adoption and was recognised under international law as protecting the child's best interests in Islamic law in the same way as adoption. In applying the relevant international conventions the respondent state had made a flexible compromise between the law of the child's country of origin and its own law, eventually helping cushion the restrictions on adoption as the child became more fully integrated into French society. Considering the margin of appreciation left to the states in the matter, the Court found no violation of Article 8.

In *Pini and Others v. Romania*[200] an Italian couple complained about the failure of the Romanian authorities to execute court decisions concerning their adoption of two Romanian children. Namely, the private institution in which the children resided in Romania had refused to hand them over and the children themselves did not wish to go with the applicants and sought revocation of the adoption. Considering the

---

198. *Ageyevy v. Russia*, No. 7075/10, 18 April 2013.
199. *Harroudj v. France*, No. 43631/09, 4 October 2012.
200. *Pini and Others v. Romania*, Nos. 78028/01 and 78030/01, ECHR 2004V (extracts).

merits of the case, the Court interpreted Article 8 in light of the UNCRC and the Hague Convention on Protection of Children and Co-operation in respect of Intercountry Adoption. The Court concluded that the positive obligation on the authorities to enable the applicants to establish family ties with their adopted children was circumscribed by the best interests of the child. In finding that there had been no violation of Article 8, the Court emphasised that in a relationship based on adoption it was important that the child's interests prevail over those of the parents, since adoption meant providing a child with a family, not a family with a child.

Child abduction

A particularly detailed elaboration of the best interests of the child has been offered in cases concerning wrongful abduction of children within the meaning of the Hague Convention on the Civil Aspects of International Abduction of Children. Inspired by a desire to protect children, regarded as the first victims of the trauma caused by their removal to, or retention in, another country by one of their parents, the Hague Convention seeks to deter the proliferation of international child abductions. It is therefore a matter, once the conditions for the application of the Hague Convention have been met, of restoring as soon as possible the status quo ante in order to avoid the legal consolidation of *de facto* situations that were brought about wrongfully, and of leaving the issues of custody and parental authority to be determined by the courts that have jurisdiction in the place of the child's habitual residence.

However, in recent cases the Court was faced with resolving situations in which the return of the child to the requesting state might expose him or her to physical or psychological harm. In those cases the Court emphasised that the obligations imposed by Article 8 on the contracting states had to be interpreted in the light of the requirements of the Hague Convention and those of the UNCRC. The underlying philosophy of all three instruments revolved around the best interests of the child. Thus, requests for return under the Hague Convention could not be ordered automatically or mechanically without evaluating the best interests of the child in the light of the exceptions provided for by the Hague Convention itself, notably the one in Article 13.*b* concerning "grave risk that the child's return would expose him to physical or psychological harm or otherwise place him in an intolerable situation". The child's best interests depend on a variety of individual circumstances, in particular age and level of maturity, the presence or absence of his or her parents as well as environment and experiences and had to be assessed in each individual case by the national authorities of the requested state.

In *Neulinger and Shuruk v. Switzerland*[201] the mother refused to return with her son to his father in Israel, where they had lived all together prior to her arrival in Switzerland. The Court stated that domestic courts had to conduct an in-depth examination of the complete family situation and of an entire series of factors, in particular of a factual, emotional, psychological, material and medical nature, and make a balanced and reasonable assessment of the respective interests of each person, with a constant concern for determining what the best solution would be for the abducted child in

---

201. *Neulinger and Shuruk v. Switzerland* [GC], No. 41615/07, ECHR 2010.

the context of an application for his return to his country of origin. In the concrete circumstances of the case that meant leaving the child with his mother in Switzerland due to, *inter alia*, the significant disturbance that his forced return to Israel would be likely to cause.

In *X. v. Latvia*[202] the Court clarified this obligation stating that when assessing an application for a child's return, domestic courts did not only need to consider arguable allegations of a "grave risk" for the child in the event of return, but also had to make a ruling, giving specific reasons in the light of the specific circumstances of the case. Both a refusal to take account of objections to the return capable of falling within the scope of one of the exception clauses of the Hague Convention or insufficient reasoning by the court dismissing such objections would be contrary to the requirements of Article 8 of the Convention as well as to the aim and purpose of the Hague Convention itself. In the present case the competent court had failed to take into consideration a psychologist's certificate attesting that the immediate separation of the child from her mother was to be ruled out on account of the likelihood of psychological trauma.

Conclusion

In conclusion, the European Court of Human Rights has consistently acknowledged the principle confirmed in Article 3 UNCRC that the best interests of the child must be a primary consideration in all cases concerning children. The Court is sometimes criticised for not defining clear criteria to consider when assessing the best interests of the child. However, such criticism does not seem entirely justified.

On the one hand, the Court has accepted that identification of the child's best interests and the assessment of the overall proportionality of any given measure require courts to weigh a number of factors in the balance. In *Y.C. v. the United Kingdom*[203] the Court admitted that it had never set out an exhaustive list of such factors, which may vary depending on the circumstances of the case in question. However, it concluded that the considerations listed in relevant domestic provisions broadly reflected the various elements inherent in assessing the necessity under Article 8 of a measure placing a child for adoption. In particular, in seeking to identify the best interests of a child and in assessing the necessity of any proposed measure in the context of placement proceedings, the domestic court had to demonstrate that it has had regard to, *inter alia*, the age, maturity and ascertained wishes of the child, the likely effect on the child of ceasing to be a member of his or her original family and the relationship the child has with relatives.

Furthermore, in a custody case *Schmidt v. France*[204] the Court set out some of the factors underlying the notion of the best interests of the child, emphasising in particular that the contracting states of the Convention should act to protect the child's psychological balance and development, well-being, health, rights and freedoms. These are to a large extent compatible with elements set out in General Comment

---

202. *X v. Latvia* [GC], No. 27853/09, ECHR 2013.
203. *Y.C. v. the United Kingdom*, No. 4547/10, 13 March 2012.
204. *Schmidt v. France*, No. 35109/02, 26 July 2007.

No. 14, adopted by the UN Committee on the Rights of the Child some five years after the delivery of the Court's judgment in the above case. Moreover, in light of that General Comment to the UNCRC, of which the Court takes particular note in children's rights cases, as well as the fact that the criteria to be taken into account are in any event not uniform and might differ in each particular case, it does not appear necessary for the Court to come up with its own list of criteria. On the other hand, it might at times be desirable for the Court to give more attention to, or explanation of, what it considers to be in the best interests of the child in a particular case – as it has done in cases referred to throughout this article.

It is in the first place for the national authorities to assess and take into consideration the best interests of the child in all matters concerning children. The task of the Court – when and if the case comes before it – is to consider those findings in the light of the Convention bearing in mind other relevant international instruments in the field, such as the UNCRC.

How can we ensure that the best interests of the child are a primary consideration in social work?

Cristina Martins
President of the International Federation of Social Workers, European Region

The best interests of the child and children's rights in general are a main concern for social workers who work with children. The United Nations Convention on the Rights of the Child (UNCRC) sets the essential standards that all those working with children must respect, including essential aspects of children's care and treatment.

Social workers have the responsibility to promote social justice, in relation to society in general and in relation to the people with whom they work. Human rights are inseparable from social work theory, values, ethics and practice, which is why advocacy of human rights is an integral part of social work.

The challenges social workers face in their decision making concerning children are various. Organisations such as the International Federation of Social Workers (IFSW) can help individual social workers cope with these challenges. The IFSW is a global organisation striving for social justice, human rights and social development through the promotion of social work, best practice models and the facilitation of international co-operation. The IFSW has a European regional division that represents the social work profession in the Council of Europe. Common social work standards that respect human rights are essential, which is why IFSW is striving towards their attainment in day-to-day professional practice. An important goal is to ensure that all new social workers are familiar with these standards and know how to implement them in practice.

An integral part of the work of the IFSW is training social workers to better take human rights into account in their daily work. This awareness-raising work includes, for instance, developing different kinds of training manuals. IFSW contributed in creating a training manual for schools of social work and the social work profession on human rights and social work, published by the United Nations in 1992 and reprinted in 1994. That manual has been an inspiration for many, and is still used around the world. The manual discusses UN human rights instruments as well as ways in which they affect the responsibilities of social workers.[205]

---

205. United Nations (1994), *Human Rights and Social Work. A manual for Schools of Social Work and the Social Work Profession.*

The IFSW has identified five ideas that are central for social workers from a children's rights perspective. These ideas resonate with the general principles of the UNCRC. First, children have to be accepted as being, not only becoming; even though they are evolving, they enjoy their human rights from birth. Second, childhood has to be considered valuable as such; it is not only a stage towards adulthood. Third, children are active agents of their own lives, and children's views must be respected. Fourth, children must not be discriminated because of their age. Fifth, social workers have to pay attention to the special vulnerability of children.

The IFSW has also invested in developing training materials specifically related to children's rights. Even though the human rights training manual refers to children's rights, more specific instructions were needed because of the many dimensions of the UNCRC. In 2002, IFSW published a professional training manual on the UNCRC entitled *Social Work and the Rights of the Child – A Professional Training Manual on the UN Convention*.[206] The manual was created to provide stimulation and guidance to social workers, social work students and educators, as well as colleagues in related fields. The aim of the training manual was to ensure that children's human rights, as set out in the UNCRC, are fully respected and implemented within the context of social work.

The manual has four objectives: first, to promote knowledge, understanding and awareness of the rights of children and of social justice among social workers, students, teaching staff and others involved in social care; second, to provide case examples so that those using the manual can apply the convention to their everyday social work practice; third, to introduce some of the dilemmas posed by the convention, including the potential for tension between children's rights and adult's rights; and fourth, to encourage the users of the manual to develop their own contribution in order to monitor and to advance the implementation of the UNCRC at micro and macro levels. It analyses different articles of the UNCRC, including the general principles of the Convention, and their connection to social work.

The manual states that the full implementation of the concept of the best interests of the child would radically transform how societies perceive and treat children. Problems related to the current implementation are identified, as well; these include that participation rights safeguarded by Article 12 of the UNCRC are often overlooked, and that many existing processes are affected by economic constraints and are not child friendly. In individual cases, social workers need to be aware of developmental psychology and understand that the interests of the child may collide with interests of other parties. Social workers should also stay objective when describing a child's situation to authorities, for instance in court proceedings. The manual also mentions intercountry adoption and problems related to it.

What can a social worker, then, do in order to better implement the concept of the best interests of the child? When looking at children as a group, social workers can focus on organising different kinds of activities that benefit children. On a population level, the manual on social work and children's rights highlights the importance of establishing ombudsperson institutions to monitor the implementation of the UNCRC.

---

206. IFSW, *Social Work and the Rights of the Child*.

Overall, children's rights should have a larger part in decision making. Research and awareness raising can play a significant role in this.

My own professional experience as a social worker has taken place in different health institutions in Portugal. I have been working for over 20 years in the Portuguese Institute of Oncology of Porto, namely in the Oncology Paediatric Service. Health institutions have a central role in identifying different risks in children's lives, since they are very often the place where situations of children at risk or in danger are identified for the first time.

Social work interventions by the Institute of Oncology Paediatric Service aim to contribute to a better quality of life for the child patient and his or her family through social advocacy, in order to provide the support needed to face the illness and to ensure that the rights of services users are met and their voices heard. It also works to provide the support needed to face any problematic situation that is identified.

In Portugal, the Supporting Children and Youth at Risk Teams have the mission of intervening when the physical, mental and social well-being of any child user of a health institution is or may be in danger, so that legal proceedings are taken, in close collaboration with the Project for Family and Children Support (Projecto de Apoio à Família e à Criança, PAFAC). Each team consists of one doctor who co-ordinates the intervention, one nurse, one social worker, one psychologist and one legal expert. The teams receive guidance from the Directorate General of Health's Monitoring Commission for the Health Action for Children and Youth at Risk, and one of its tasks is the promotion of the rights of children and youth.

The Portuguese law on protection of children in danger (Lei de Protecção das Crianças em Perigo) provides an important tool for social workers to identify situations in which children may be in danger. According to this law, an intervention must occur when the parent (or other legal guardian) endangers a child's safety, health, training, education or development, or when this danger results from an action or omission of third parties or of the child, to which they do not object properly. The intervention has to be based on, among other factors, the principle of the best interests of the child.

Finally, I would like to bring forward three important issues I have encountered in my own work in the paediatric service. First, social workers need to be firmly supported by legal mechanisms in their daily practice while advocating for and ensuring the best interests of the child. Even with the best protective laws, existence of legal mechanisms and well-trained teams, social workers may not find enough means, tools and resources to achieve the best for the children they are working for.

There is thus a need for stronger prevention measures and policies supported by adequate financial and human resources. Sometimes the lack of the most adequate response to the needs of the child can limit the social work intervention and the professional's view and decision on the best interests of the child (health institutions normally provide the first safe home for children at risk but this should be only for a transitional period).

Second, a social worker who works to ensure the best interests of the child needs a lot of courage. He or she may have to fight some battles on the way, while advocating and working for the protection of the child in danger. This can include conflicts with family members who are abusing the child, institutional personnel, community members and others. I would say that courage, determination and special training are absolutely necessary to deal properly with the demanding nature of our work.

Third, there is the question of whether social workers should be more prominent in their action as political agents to make a difference for the best interests of the child. My positive answer to this question comes without hesitation. Why an absolute "yes"? Social worker practitioners have great experience in dealing with children at risk. They are able to use their knowledge of social work practice in the research they perform. Through this, they can develop methods for future social work practice. Social work can bring social analysis, social catalyst and social action to different situations. The first helps people understand, the second helps people achieve change for themselves and the third happens through social relationships to sustain change.[207] IFSW Europe encourages social workers to be more active by underlining the problems they face in their daily practice and using their knowledge and expertise to propose changes in policies than can better protect children in society.

The problem, however, is that many social workers face serious limitations when putting their knowledge into action. Their lack of time to write and to engage in extra activities due to the amount of tasks and responsibilities that they already have during their daily work limits them. This situation is more deeply felt by professionals from the countries most affected by the economic and social crisis and austerity measures adopted in response to it. In these countries, the workload of social workers is increasing; many work more hours a day with less pay, which affects their professional performance.

In conclusion, I would like to underline the importance of keeping one's professional skills up to date. Social workers should also follow practice based on evidence and current knowledge. In their daily work, social workers often face difficulties while trying to protect children from all forms of violence, neglect and abuse. There is a need for stronger prevention measures and policies, supported by adequate financial and human resources. In the current economic situation we cannot set our hopes too high, but we must however stick to the standards we have.

It is also absolutely necessary to work in multidisciplinary teams to be sure that a proper evaluation of each case is made. After identifying the risk, the social worker needs to be prepared to activate the proper mechanism to report the abuse. It is very important to be very sure about what he or she is reporting and stay objective, as the consequences of a false alarm can cause harm. It would also help social workers in their work if they, and service users, had a possibility to refer to a body with the legally recognised remit of safeguarding of professional ethics and providing redress.

My final remark is not a novelty in light of what I have described in this text. I find it very important to underline that while the UNCRC has changed the understanding of the rights of children and the way children are viewed and treated, much still remains to be done in practice to better ensure the rights of children all across Europe and worldwide. This is exactly the aim of social workers. Social work must be the voice of the child.

207. IFSW, _The best interests of the child_, Statement of 6 February 2009.

The best interests of the child in removal decisions – A parliamentary perspective

Valeriu Ghileţchi
Chairperson of the Committee on Social Affairs, Health and Sustainable Development of the Council of Europe Parliamentary Assembly

How can we make sure that the best interests of the child are fully respected when deciding about removing children from their families? This problem has become more and more important in recent years in many member states of the Council of Europe. According to Article 9 of the United Nations Convention on the Rights of the Child (UNCRC), a child shall not be separated from his or her parents against their will, except when such separation is necessary in the best interests of the child. In other words, the best interests of the child serve as a determining criterion in decision making. The best interests of the child must be put first when a removal decision is taken – usually by social services – to remove a child from his or her family.

The complexity of the question of best interests in removal decisions derives from the twofold nature of the problem. Sometimes children are left in abusive families and not taken into care quickly enough – or not taken into care at all – whereas sometimes removal decisions are taken too rashly or are unwarranted. Both the lack of an intervention and an unnecessary intervention can constitute a serious breach of children's rights. Children have the right to be protected from violence, abuse and neglect, but they also have the right not to be separated from their parents. It is not enough to show that a child could be placed in a more beneficial upbringing environment to remove a child from his or her family.

In April 2015, the Council of Europe Parliamentary Assembly adopted Resolution 2049 and Recommendation 2068, "Social services in Europe: legislation and practice of the removal of children from their families in Council of Europe member States". The report at the origin of these texts, drawn up by rapporteur Olga Borzova from Russia, discusses children's rights in the context of removal decisions.

The Committee on Social Affairs, Health and Sustainable Development of the Council of Europe Parliamentary Assembly worked on the report for approximately two years. The rapporteur undertook three fact-finding visits – to Finland, Romania and the United Kingdom – in order to better prepare the report. The Committee also received 30 replies to a parliamentary research questionnaire on legislation and practice of the removal of children from their families. Relevant judgments of the European Court of Human Rights and documents of the United Nations Committee on the Rights of the Child were also taken into account in the drafting of the report.

The Committee on Social Affairs, Health and Sustainable Development first set out to establish whether there had been an increase in unwarranted removal decisions in Council of Europe member states. The next question was whether there was a pattern to these decisions: are migrant parents, parents belonging to national minorities or minority religious groups or from poor socio-economic backgrounds disproportionately victims of such unwarranted removal decisions? Should this be the case, how could national laws or implementing guidelines be changed in order to improve decision making at the level of the social services, with a view to guaranteeing the rights of children and parents alike, while effectively protecting children? Fourth, the report aimed at identifying good practices in member states that could serve as an inspiration for other member states and help them develop their own good practices.

In answering these questions, the Committee considered that a misunderstanding (and sometimes abuse) of the concept of the best interests of the child is one of the main factors in unwarranted removal decisions. At the same time, the best interests of the child should be the cornerstone of all removal decisions. The concept of the best interests of the child has had a prominent role in many legal texts and recommendations since its inclusion in the UNCRC in 1989. The concept is also one of the most widely misunderstood concepts of this convention, as the Committee on the Rights of the Child has lamented frequently in its reports, which led it to issue its General Comment No. 14 (2013) on the right of the child to have his or her best interests taken as a primary consideration (Article 3.1).

In this General Comment, the Committee on the Rights of the Child considers that the principle of the best interests of the child should be applied in a way that not only laws and regulations, but also the actors on the ground (in this case social services), truly put the best interests of the child first in removal, placement and reunification decisions. The Committee also stated in the General Comment that a child should only be separated from his or her parents as a measure of last resort, and that separation should not take place if less intrusive measures could protect the child. The Committee equally declared that it is "indispensable" to carry out an assessment and determination of the child's best interests in the context of a potential separation of a child from his or her parents.[208]

The report of the Parliamentary Assembly found that national legislation in most countries of the Council of Europe complies with international law. The bar for the

___
208. UN Committee on the Rights of the Child, General Comment No. 14 (2013) on the right of the child to have his or her best interests taken as a primary consideration, paragraphs 58-61.

decision of social services to remove a child from the family is generally quite a high one in all Council of Europe member states, usually involving the concept of serious harm. The majority of countries that answered the questionnaire take removal decisions based on serious harm having occurred, the imminent risk of serious harm or the risk of serious harm (although the exact wording may differ from country to country). The definition of what constitutes serious harm differs from state to state, and has often evolved over time to include not just physical abuse, but also sexual, emotional or psychological abuse. Some countries add further possible motives such as "economic violence", a child committing a criminal offence or using drugs or other toxic substances, or a child being beyond parental control. In almost all cases, the final decision to take a child into care is subject to judicial decision.

The number of children taken into care varies widely from country to country. The report classed states into three categories according to the percentage of the child population in care: low (below .5%), medium (up to .8%) and high range (up to 1.66%). However, since many replies furnished only total numbers (not percentages in relation to the size of the child population in the country), it was sometimes difficult to judge whether the number of children taken into care is in the low, medium or high range. Only a few countries gather statistics on the ethnic or religious minority status, immigrant status or socio-economic background of children taken into care. Most countries place children with relatives or foster families or in public or private institutions. More rarely, children are given up for adoption.

Even though direct comparisons were not possible due to the ambiguity of the data available, some conclusions could be made. The report found that, on the one hand, in some countries (or regions thereof) social services take some children into care too rashly, and do not make enough effort to support families before and/or after removal and placement decisions. These unwarranted decisions usually have a – sometimes unintended – discriminatory character to them, and can constitute serious violations of the rights of the child and his or her parents, all the more tragic when the decisions are irreversible (such as in the cases of adoption without parental consent).

On the other hand, in some countries (or regions thereof) social services do not take children into care quickly enough, or return children too rashly to abusive or neglectful parental care. These decisions can constitute equally – or more – serious violations of the rights of the child, and can put a child's life and health in danger.

Based on the report, the Parliamentary Assembly adopted a resolution with key recommendations concerning removal decisions and the best interests of the child. I will discuss here in detail the recommendations I find the most central. First of all, it is necessary to make visible and root out the influence of prejudice and discrimination in removal decisions, including by appropriately training all professionals involved. Professionals are human too, and – particularly in the wake of highly publicised cases of children dying at the hands of their parents – there is going to be a lot of pressure for social workers to err on the side of caution. Unfortunately, being human, we are all influenced by stereotypes, and depending on the situation in a particular country, we may feel that it is more likely that, for example, poor and uneducated families, or foreigners, or families belonging to a minority, will treat their children badly. The European Court of Human Rights has underlined that it is in the child's best interests that his or her family ties should be maintained except in cases where the family has proved to be particularly unfit. According to the Court, family ties may only be severed in very exceptional circumstances and everything must be done to preserve personal relations and, where appropriate, to "rebuild" the family. It is not enough to show that a child could be placed in a more beneficial environment for his or her upbringing.[209]

Second, families need to be supported in an appropriate way (including financially and materially) in order to avoid the necessity for removal decisions in the first place, and in order to increase the percentage of successful family reunifications after care. To take an extreme example given by Olga Borzova, the rapporteur of the Committee on Social Affairs, Health and Sustainable Development, the solution for a hungry child is not to take him or her into care, but to ensure that the child's family has the resources to feed the child.

Third, there are some practices which should be avoided when it comes to removal decisions, except in exceptional circumstances. These are severing family ties completely, removing children from parental care at birth, basing placement decisions on the effluxion of time, and having recourse to adoptions without parental consent (particularly when adoptions without parental consent become irreversible).

Fourth, it is important to ensure that the personnel involved in removal and placement decisions is suitably qualified and regularly trained, has sufficient resources to take decisions in an appropriate timeframe, and is not overburdened with a too high caseload.

Fifth and finally, we need better data collection. Anonymised data should be collected on the care population in member states. This data should be disaggregated not only by age and gender, and alternative care type, but also by ethnic minority status, immigrant status and socio-economic background, as well as by length of time spent in care until family reunification. By collecting this kind of data, we would have a clearer picture of how we can better help children who need our protection, while also better protecting the rights of the birth families.

I believe that only when these recommendations are implemented will we have really put the best interests of the child first. I would like to call on all Council of Europe member states to implement the recommendations contained in Resolution 2049 (2015), and on the Committee of Ministers and its subordinate bodies to work on the guidelines we urgently need on this matter, as demanded in Recommendation 2068 (2015).

---

209. *Y.C. v. the United Kingdom*, No. 4547/10, 13 March 2012, paragraph 134.

Children's perspectives concerning imprisonment: setting up a self-expression group of children with imprisoned parents or other relatives

Mentoring and support for maintaining family ties in accordance with the child's best interests

Astrid Hirschelmann

Lecturer, qualified to direct psychological and criminological research, University of Rennes 2

Imprisonment is a complex issue which may lead prisoners' families and others close to them to become withdrawn and uncommunicative, and possibly to conceal the real reasons for their absence due to the associated social opprobrium. Imprisonment is first and foremost a social response to crime, and children's best interests have so far been given scant consideration in this context. Indeed, children are all too often part of the "collateral damage" of adults' actions and decisions.

The concept of a child's best interests requires us to heed the way in which the child experiences the situation of a parent's or other relative's imprisonment and to gauge its impact on the quality of their affectional bond. It is important to help the child express what he or she is experiencing and to propose a plan of action or support for the family only as a second step, once its members' wishes and capabilities for maintaining or building ties have been evaluated. If due consideration is not given to the position of the members of the family concerned, forcibly cultivating the bond can be as harmful as breaking it. It has to be acknowledged that at present not enough is known about how a child feels in this situation and what repercussions this experience can have on his/her development and personal and social fulfilment. Consequently, our adult projections may be at odds with the child's interests.

The surveys conducted by UFRAMA[210] (2008, 2012) give a particularly good indication of all the difficulties encountered by families in coming to terms with the imprisonment of a parent or relative. These questions are even more complicated when children are involved, and the most recent UFRAMA survey (2012) showed that 50% of children aged 2 to 5 and 23% of those aged 5 to 9 are not informed "explicitly" of their parent's imprisonment; however, a majority are aware of this situation. Most of the time they are therefore in a difficult position coupled with an inability to talk about it.

As a result, very little is known about how children experience a family member's imprisonment. This lack of knowledge leaves room for all kinds of projections, which can victimise and more generally stigmatise these children. What hinders their development may not be so much the situation of imprisonment as the repercussions of the stigma and misconceptions it fosters among people in the child's more or less immediate environment. The project "Regards d'enfants sur l'incarcération: mise en place d'un groupe d'expression d'enfants de parents ou proches incarcérés" (RESI) (Children's perspectives concerning imprisonment: setting up a self-expression group of children with imprisoned parents or other relatives) is a research project which was conducted by the city of Rennes from January 2013 to January 2015.[211] Carried out by the Centre Interdisciplinaire d'Analyse des Processus Humains et Sociaux[212] and by the organisations Brin de Soleil[213] and Enjeux d'Enfants,[214] the RESI project set out to create and test a new support system in the form of a self-expression group intended for children with an imprisoned parent or close relative.

Research into risk and crime prevention shows how important it is to look after a child's development and well-being early on. Without going to the opposite extreme where children are almost invariably considered as victims, we deemed it

---

210. Union des fédérations régionales des maisons d'accueil de familles et amis de personnes incarcérées (Union of regional federations of reception centres for families and friends of imprisoned persons).

211. The RESI project was conducted with the financial support of Rennes 2 University, the National Observatory of Endangered Children, the Brittany Region and the Fondation de France.

212. The CIAPHS, Interdisciplinary Centre for Analysis of Human and Social Processes, is an academic Équipe d'accueil (Hosting Team) (EA 2241) recognised under a five-year contract 2012-2017 and placed under the supervision of Rennes 2 University. The team's remit is to initiate programmes and conduct interdisciplinary research work concerning four thematic areas: "Development", "Integration", "Violence" and "Language". The team brings together jurists, sociologists, economists, managers, linguists and psychologists on common, transversal topics. This multidisciplinary perspective is intended to stimulate a renewal of approaches and cross-fertilisation of procedures, enabling the team to build theoretical frameworks conducive to academic work and the fulfilment of social demands for research.

213. The Brin de soleil organisation comprises three reception centres for families and friends of imprisoned persons. Arc-en-ciel accommodates families from far away for a stay of three days maximum; Ti Tomm and Luciole offer support before and after prison visits, respectively at the Rennes-Vezin men's prison and the Rennes women's prison.

214. According to its articles, the association Enjeux d'Enfants proposes support by all the appropriate means for the relationship between a child and his or her imprisoned parent or any other imprisoned person with whom the child has maintained affectional or educational bonds, or vice versa between an imprisoned child and his or her parent or another person with whom the child has maintained affectional or educational bonds, where they are entitled to visits. In particular, it arranges adapted visits for imprisoned parents and their children, where appropriate, escorted visits in prison visiting facilities and/or in a Family Life Unit (UVF) and organises children's travel to their accommodation.

important to restore their rightful place simply by giving them the right to express themselves, so as to better adapt our interventions while respecting their emotional balance. In France, self-expression groups for children and adolescents are still rare, and they tend to favour a mentoring approach to the existential consequences of broken family ties, sometimes at the risk of overlooking the individual psychological processes behind these rifts.

The RESI self-expression group allows children to show where they stand concerning the situation imposed on them and how they can respond to it for themselves, at least for the time being, and also and most importantly with reference to "others" (within their social, intra-family and extra-family environment). The technical consequence of this methodological approach to the conduct of the RESI sessions was to combine a non-directive ("projective") proposal of topics for each session with a stance of more directive stimulus and insistence ("guidance") recalling that these topics are only different aspects of a problem which is central and is kept that way by the "moderators". This enables each of the children, within and through the group, and via these topics, to try out responses to the central problem being worked on – namely, "Daddy (or Mummy, or any other relative) is in prison".

The topics of the five proposed sessions, and their sequence, correspond to a progressive variation on the general, guiding theme of the series worked on by the RESI group. They include:

Session 1: "What does prison mean for you?"

This assignment, involving both verbal interaction and practical work, introduces the theme of prison and proposes it to the children as a recapitulation of their reason for participating in this group (implicitly, they have an experience of prison due to their respective family situations, and the group has been presented to them more or less as a time and place "where it is possible to talk about prison"). Moreover, this assignment is formulated in the plural ("vous"), which straightway emphasises that the children will need to try and answer this question in a collective context (the group), or even as a collective entity (children with the common attribute of having an imprisoned parent).

Session 2: "The imagined prison: how would you like prison to be?"

This second theme may appear surprising at first since prison is not ostensibly a place that lends itself to an imagined "ideal". It is presented to the children as a game about what they would like to change in the prison, and it is presumed that they will be more receptive to the idea as they have a real, experience-based knowledge of prison (they are children who have an imprisoned parent). In a playful and positive manner, the children in the RESI group are thus confronted with the very concept of imprisonment: "What does it mean to imprison someone (or to put someone in prison)? What does it mean to be imprisoned (or to be, to live, in prison)?" This assignment implicitly asks the children about their "understanding", as credited to them by others and/or by themselves, of the fact of imprisoning/being imprisoned where the "prisoner" is their parent, and also about the "empathy" credited to them by others and/or by themselves with regard to this imprisoned parent.

Session 3: "What is it like to live in the absence of an imprisoned parent?"

This third assignment involves more practical work than verbal interaction, since it consists in preparing pictures and showing them to the children in the group, each of whom is asked to choose one or more of these pictures and to tell a related story, *within* and *to* the group. The pictures were devised by the research team and produced in close collaboration with two graphic artists and professional illustrators, Jean Bossard and Pierre Ramine, especially for the RESI research project. The aspect of the RESI scheme's cardinal concerns being addressed here is that of separation from the imprisoned parent and the consequences of this absence and/or of subsequent regulated visits or communications.

Session 4: "The moment of separation"

Here too, the assignment is more practical, and even action-oriented, than verbal, since it takes the form of a game with puppets centred on the parent's apprehension by the authorities. The puppets were chosen by the research team to best serve this purpose. The central concern being raised with the children in the group is approached from the angle of the "shock" caused by the intervention of the justice system in their lives, and the consequences of this shock for each of them but also and above all for their respective environments, with knock-on effects on themselves and their position in relation to this critical and possibly traumatic situation.

Session 5: "Conclusion(s) and feedback for the RESI sequence"

This fifth session was identified from the outset as the last in the RESI sequence (in the context of its research-oriented experiment), and intended to serve the objective of a final reconstitution for and with the parents. Again, the children are appealed to as a group (reinforced by the fact that no one else is permitted to join the scheme after session 4), so as to produce a common, "publishable" conclusion intended for the parents. At the very least, this might be conceived as a preparation for the parents'"return" to the RESI scheme, in the form of a concluding collective tea party to which they are invited all together, both as guests and contributors.

The results of this research consolidate the idea that such a scheme is useful, nevertheless it was not easy to set up. Although the children quickly took possession of this facility dedicated to them, the research team had to come to terms with a certain inertia or hesitation on the part of the professionals assisting the families, as well as with positively or negatively idealised projections and passive resistance by the parents. These reactions are undoubtedly due to the novelty of the arrangement, but also reveal anxieties about professional boundaries, the right to intrude on the privacy of families, and more generally the lack of a network or linkage of the work carried out with the families.

Regarding the children involved in the RESI scheme experiment, it was indeed possible to observe some of the forecast familial impediments, but not always those which might have been expected. All the children immediately accepted the proposed guiding theme for the group ("Daddy [or Mummy] is in prison"), without showing any major or prohibitive opposition. They took ownership of the scheme and were able to position themselves within it according to their individual situations and sensitivities. The varied nature of these reactions and of their development despite the low number of sessions shows that this scheme is effective and adaptable to a "case-by-case" approach in the common operational framework of work within and by a peer group.

For instance, thanks to the group, one of the children emerged from a state of social and family isolation linked to his mother's imprisonment by permitting the other younger children in the group to benefit from his better-informed knowledge of the prison environment. A little later, the same child was able to express doubts about his personal value in the eyes of others and of his own family. Another child in the group was able to voice her concerns over the conditions of her father's imprisonment and his well-being in prison. Since she expressed a very negative perception of the prison guards, confusedly described by her as "policemen", and suspected them of malice towards her father, a discussion ensued among the children concerning the prison guards' work and what each child knew about them.

Two limitations to this globally positive response nevertheless emerged: firstly, the unsuitability of the scheme for children under 5 or 6 (the very young age of one of the children made it difficult for him to participate in certain assignments); secondly, the possibility of a participant requesting psychological help in one form or another following this experience with a self-expression group (one of the children plainly expressed his interest in the work of self-expression proposed and his regret over the termination of the group and the limited number of sessions).

The recommendations formulated at the end of this research project emphasise the importance of a community-based approach to aid the families and relatives of prisoners, geared to the different levels of the family group. To be able to work with a child, it is necessary to work with the whole family group and win their trust, which cannot be done without solidarity and partnership among the different players and professional structures dealing with the family. And to make this partnership work possible, the professionals need to be able to identify clearly their partners' tasks and roles, as well as to agree on the information that can or should be shared.

The child's best interests and the right to know his or her origins[215]

Géraldine Mathieu
Lecturer, University of Namur, Belgium; projects officer for Defence of Children International (DCI-Belgium)

Deceiving a child about his parentage can drive him mad.[216]

When I was born, my mother abandoned me in absolute anonymity. On my birth certificate there is a large cross, an "X" in place of my mother's name. I do not hold it against her. I would just like to know why she didn't want me…

I was adopted abroad. I would like to consult my adoption file, to know my history, to know which orphanage I grew up in before coming here, because I remember nothing. I would also like to find my mother again, to know whether I have brothers and sisters. I often think of her, of them; even if I don't know them, they are part of me.

I resemble neither my father nor my mother, everyone in the family makes me aware of it. This puts me ill at ease, I no longer know what to think. I believe I was conceived by medically assisted procreation. Whenever I meet a man resembling me in the street, I feel like accosting him to find out whether by chance he was a sperm donor at one time. I feel I am going mad.

I was born of a surrogate mother, everyone around me knows it. But my parents refuse to tell me who this woman is who carried me for nine months and is often in my thoughts. I would very much like to be able to thank her.

I was born as a result of artificial insemination, my girlfriend too. We are afraid we might be the offspring of the same donor. What will happen if we have a child? And can we marry?

---

215. European Conference on the Best Interests of the Child, Brussels, 9 and 10 December 2014, summing-up of workshop No. 8. Further reading: Mathieu G. (2014), *Le secret des origines en droit de la filiation*, Doctoral thesis, Wolters Kluwer Waterloo.

216. Rousseau D. (2012), *Les grandes personnes sont vraiment stupides. Ce que nous apprennent les enfants en détresse*, Max Milo Publications, Paris, p. 11.

I don't know my father, he left my mother before I was born. My mother refuses to tell me who he is. I have a good idea who, but the man I suspect of being my father refuses to undergo a DNA test to check what kind of tie we have. This rejection is terribly painful for me. I so badly need recognition by this man, even of a purely token kind, to exist in his eyes, to exist at all…

How can we know who we are when we do not know where we come from? While enquiry into one's origins is nothing new, never has it been so forcefully pursued. Compelled by studies in the social and psychological sciences, the question of the search for origins now prompts numerous debates in the legal world too,[217] and an effective demand for a right to access one's origins is being witnessed. This is undoubtedly one of the most sensitive societal debates in the last 20 years,[218] one which recurs in matters of adoption, anonymous childbirth, medically assisted procreation, surrogate motherhood, DNA profiling or even the prohibition of incest.

Can a legislator deny a person the knowledge of where he or she comes from? Should a regulatory instrument expressly recognise and guarantee each individual's right to know his or her maternal and paternal origins? Should this right also be internationally enshrined? And how, in this context, can the different contending interests be ranked: each person's interest in knowing the truth about his or her origins, the parents' interest in having a child whatever the circumstances, a third party's interest in remaining anonymous, a woman's interest in not disclosing her identity at childbirth?

Searching for one's origins is inseparable from every human being's reflection on his or her personal identity, which makes a person an individual, distinct from other individuals but intimately linked with them. This quest for identity may take on a very special significance when one's origins are obscured. The existence – or suspicion – of a secret inflames the need to know; the secrecy surrounding origins is no exception to this rule.

Whatever the original event which led to this secrecy concerning origins, it can engender real psychological distress and deal a fatal blow to self-esteem. Psychoanalysis, for almost a hundred years, has taught us that the history of our early life and the circumstances of our origins are imprinted on us, and that what is left unsaid about origins and one's life story quite simply prevents a child from thinking and ushers in a future of suffering.[219]

Anyone who feels the need – there cannot indeed be an obligation to know one's origins – should therefore be able to discover where he or she comes from, who his or her birth parents are, what his or her history is. Love for adoptive parents, those who have had recourse to gamete donation, for a single mother, however great, can never fulfil the need to understand where one comes from. Our origins are part of us; they build our personalities and are embodied in our identity. To deny a child knowledge of his or her origins is to remove a part of him or her. The most important

---

217. Meier Ph. and Stettler M. (2014), *Droit de la filiation*, 5th edition, Schulthess, Geneva, p. 241.

218. A reality TV show on the search for origins by children born through artificial insemination – *Génération Cryo* – was even made on MTV in the autumn of 2013.

219. Verdier P. (1995), "Né sous X", in Cahiers de Maternologie – L'accouchement "sous X" en question, No. 5, p. 78.

thing for a child is probably to know that the information is stored somewhere, not deliberately concealed, and always accessible when he or she wants to know.

The United Nations Convention on the Rights of the Child secures for the child (a person under 18) the right to know his or her parents, as far as possible (Article 7), and requires states to safeguard his or her identity (Article 8), but the way in which these two articles are drafted unfortunately leaves some latitude to states.

The United Nations Committee on the Rights of the Child has nevertheless had repeated opportunities to recall that states parties cannot deliberately deny a child the right to know his or her origins. In its Final Comments on France delivered in June 2004, the Committee recommended:

that the State party take all appropriate measures to ensure that the provisions of article 7, especially the right of the child to know, as far as possible, his or her parents, be fully enforced in the light of the principles of non-discrimination (art. 2) and the best interests of the child (art. 3)".[220]

In March 2005, it urgently requested Luxembourg to:

take all necessary measures to prevent and eliminate the practice of so-called anonymous childbirth. If this practice were to continue, it would be up to the State Party to take the necessary measures for all information on the parents to be recorded and archived so that the child is able, as far as possible and at the appropriate time, to know the identity of its father and/or mother.[221]

In March 2005 also, the Committee recommended that Austria "undertake all necessary measures to prevent the use of the so-called 'baby flaps'" and:

introduce and implement legal provisions and regulations for the separate registration of all relevant medical and other data, in particular the name and date of birth of the parent(s) and allow the child at an appropriate time to have access to these data.[222]

As to the Council of Europe member states, they should exercise their discretion in compliance with the obligations arising from the European Convention on Human Rights. In fact, every individual's fundamental right to respect for private life, established by Article 8 of the Convention, embraces the right to identity and personal fulfilment. On that account, it protects the legitimate interest, even termed "vital" interest by the European Court of Human Rights, of every individual (hence of the child too) in knowing his or her origins.[223] While the interest of the individual in knowing his or her origins is recognised as fundamental, the case law of the Court

---

220. Committee on the Rights of the Child, final observations on the report presented by France, No. 24, CRC/C/15/Add. 240, 2004.
221. Committee on the Rights of the Child, final observations on the report presented by Luxembourg, No. 29, CRC/C/15/Add. 250, 2005.
222. Committee on the Rights of the Child, final observations on the report presented by Austria, No. 30, CRC/C/15/Add. 251, 2005. See also Committee on the Rights of the Child, final observations on the report presented by the Czech Republic, CRC/C/CZE/CO/3-4, 2011.
223. See Mathieu G. and Willems G. (2014), "Origines, parentalité et parenté dans la jurisprudence de la Cour européenne des droits de l'homme", in Filiation, origines, parentalité, J. Sosson (ed.), Bruylant, Brussels, pp. 593-602.

indicates that it does not have an absolute character.[224] It may come into conflict with other interests which will carry more or less weight depending on the situations contemplated: the interest of the biological mother, of the mother's husband, of the biological father, of the adoptive parents, of the gamete donor, but also of the surrogate mother or siblings.

Thus it must be acknowledged that at present no international instrument expressly enshrines a person's right of access to his or her origins and that the discretion of states remains particularly wide in this area. To enhance protection of each person's fundamental right to know his or her origins, this right should be expressly and clearly enshrined at the international level, in a treaty, as well as in national constitutions.[225]

Of course there is no question of giving this right an absolute character, in the sense that it would brook no exception.[226] Other divergent interests may indeed come into conflict with the child's. The fact remains that the right to know one's origins stands out as a fundamental right that is part of human dignity. It should be limited only by way of an exception, and only if there is risk of grave prejudice for someone else.

---

224. See Mathieu 2014, pp. 110 ff.

225. Like the Swiss Constitution which acknowledges that "everyone shall have access to the data concerning his ancestry" (Article 119, paragraph 2.g of the Federal Constitution). In Germany, the Federal Constitutional Court has since 1989 secured to everyone the right to know their biological origins (BVerfG, 31 January 1989, *FamRZ*, 1989, pp. 255 ff.). The Constitutional Court infers from this two fundamental rights explicitly guaranteed by the constitution: the right to respect for dignity (Article 1.1 of the constitution) and the right to free development (Article 2.1 of the constitution).

226. There are, for that matter, very few "absolute" rights; in particular, the right to life and the right not to be tortured: indeed, no higher interest can justify violation of these rights.

Concluding remarks

What does the concept of the best interests of the child actually mean? How should it be interpreted and applied in practice? What is the added value of this concept, if there is one at all? It was to find answers to these questions that the authors of this edited volume gathered at the conference 'The best interests of the child: a dialogue between theory and practice' in Brussels in December 2014.

The contributions of this volume reflect a great diversity in approaching the concept of the best interests of the child. Many describe it as crucial and highly useful for the interpretation of the UNCRC, as long as it is properly applied. Others remind of the concept's legacy of misuse and risk of contentious application and prefer to use it as little as possible. Even though the perspectives presented in the publication are different from each other, many of the authors pay attention to same aspects of the concept of the best interests of the child. Some consider the concept more important than others, but there are a number of insights which are common to most, if not all, contributors to this volume.

It was perceived as helpful to understand the concept as having three dimensions, as suggested by General Comment No. 14 of the Committee on the Rights of the Child: the best interests of the child as a substantive right, as a legal principle and as a rule of procedure.

The first dimension refers to the *substantive right* of the child to have his or her best interests taken as a primary consideration when different interests are being considered in order to reach a decision. In this sense, Article 3.1 creates an obligation for States, is directly applicable and can be invoked before a court. This right, however, it is not superior to other rights in the UNCRC and inter-reliant with other articles of the convention. Article 3.1 should be seen as a protective article that makes sure *all rights* in the convention are protected in cases where an evaluation or a decision in a specific case has to be made. As Jorge Cardona Llorens, member of the UN Committee on the Rights of the Child, put it: The best interests of the child is not what we consider to be the best situation of the child, but what is objectively proven to be the best for the effective realisation of his or her rights. Balancing conflicting rights between a child or a group of children on the one hand and other children or adults on the other hand, is challenging. It can be difficult to find a solution that guarantees the best interests of the child or group of children, but does not violate fundamental rights of another child, other children, or adults.

The second dimension refers to the best interests of the child as a fundamental, interpretative *legal principle*. If a legal provision is open to more than one interpretation, the interpretation which most effectively serves the child's best interests should be chosen. In this respect, the vagueness of this principle is both a challenge and an opportunity. The drafters of the convention deliberately left the concept undefined so that its interpretation could take account of context and circumstances. The best interests of the child it is not a stand-alone principle and must be understood and applied in the light of other general principles of the convention, in particular Article 12 on the right of the child to be heard. There is also a strong interconnection with Article 5 (evolving capacities of the child) and Article 17 (children's access to appropriate information). Hence, one of the key messages of the conference was the need to listen to the child and to children as a group whenever a best interest assessment is undertaken.

The *procedure* defining the best interests of the child deserves particular attention. As General Comment No. 14 states, whenever a decision is to be made that will affect a specific child, an identified group of children or children in general, the decision-making process must include an evaluation of the possible impact of the decision on the child or children concerned. Several contributions provided insights into how to assess individual children's best interests on a case by case basis, by a multidisciplinary team and in close collaboration with the child. It was concluded that more efforts need to be done to develop objective criteria to found these decisions on. The non-exhaustive and non-hierarchical list of elements suggested in General Comment No. 14 was considered as a useful tool to guide the best interests determination.

There was also a broad agreement that listening to the child's views is crucial when assessing and determining the best interests. In addition to an assessment of the best interests of the child at the moment a decision is taken, it was also considered important that these decisions are subject to independent monitoring to ensure that the best interests of the child serve as a guiding principle also in the implementation of decisions.

The best interests of the child in family affairs is a particularly challenging situation because of the various interests involved – and also a situation where a child's views are essential. The conference showed that the relationship between children and their parents can be subject to severe tensions, for instance in the case of divorce, imprisonment of one of the parents, child maltreatment, a child's removal from the family, adoption or medically assisted procreation. It was found that the best interests of the child can – and should - be a compass in striking the necessary balance between different rights such as the right to maintain close ties with both parents, to know one's origins and to fully develop one's potential.

All too often, experts on the rights of the child debate with other experts on the rights of the child about the rights of the child. The conference in Brussels started to open up this academic debate to a dialogue with professionals who are applying the best interests of the child in practice. This can only be a first step, however. The theoretical debate on the best interests of the child has yet to come much closer to the professionals who apply it at a daily basis. Judges, lawyers, social workers, educators, teachers, policy makers, and many others need more space for reflection and more training on the concept of the best interests of the child.

Appendices

Appendix I – Speeches presented at the European Conference on the Best Interests of the Child – A dialogue between theory and practice
(Brussels, 9-10 December 2014)

Speech by Koen Geens, Minister of Justice, Belgium

On 20 November 2014, we celebrated the 25th anniversary of the United Nations Convention on the Rights of the Child (UNCRC). The UNCRC is the key legal instrument on children's rights. It codifies the human rights of children in an internationally binding instrument that all member states of the Council of Europe have signed and ratified.

The convention can be seen as the result of a long struggle for the recognition of children as full-fledged human beings, as subjects of rights. A quote from Janus Korczak explains why:

> Children are not the people of tomorrow, but are people of today. They have a right to be taken seriously, and to be treated with tenderness and respect. They should be allowed to grow into whoever they were meant to be – the unknown person inside each of them is our hope for the future.

The pedagogical ideas of the Polish writer, paediatrician and educator Korczak are still relevant today. For him a child is not "an unfinished human being" but a "full person" who can take initiative and responsibility. We are privileged that Ms Urszula Markowska-Manista, professor and scientific secretary of the Janusz Korczak UNESCO chair, accepted our invitation to give a presentation based on the heritage of Janus Korczak.

In the framework of the Belgian Chairmanship of the Committee of Ministers of the Council of Europe, Belgium wanted to pay particular attention to the rights of children. There are various reasons for that. The most important of them is simply that children's rights are fundamental. They originate from a demand for human dignity and social justice as human rights in general.

Instead of looking back to see what has been done and where we stand today, we chose to look forward. Therefore we put the child at the centre of our work and decided to organise a conference on the best interests of the child. The Belgian

Presidency also established the objective of promoting a true attitude change, based on the philosophy that children have to enjoy full respect and be treated as equals.

When we speak about children's rights, we should be guided by four key principles of the UNCRC: non-discrimination, the best interests of the child, survival and development, and last but not least participation. Those four principles were put forward by the UN Committee on the Rights of the Child in 1991. It is precisely one of these key principles – and perhaps also the most troubling one, the best interests of the child, that is the focus of the conference.

Laws, official documents, court rulings and decisions of social workers often state that they are in the best interests of the child. Sometimes no further explanation is offered as to why a certain decision is or is not in the best interests of the child. Academics, lawyers and field actors have been indicating for years that the concept of the best interests of the child is vague, complex and difficult to measure and evaluate. A decision which seems to be a good decision in the best interests of the child today might no longer seem to be in the best interests of the very same child in the years to come. Based on this concept, many professionals get involved in the lives of children in the name of their best interests – perhaps with the best intentions, but sometimes with disastrous consequences for the children's lives.

It is therefore with much interest that we have taken note of General Comment No. 14 of the Committee on the Rights of the Child on the right of a child to have his or her interests taken as a primary consideration (Article 3.1). The General Comment defines the requirements for a careful examination of a child's best interests and provides a framework for the evaluation and determination of the best interests of the child.

The main objective of the General Comment is to reinforce the understanding and the application of the right of children to have their best interests evaluated and to have their best interests taken as a, or in certain cases the, primary consideration. According to Article 3.1 of the UNCRC, the best interests of the child have to be a primary consideration in all cases concerning children. In addition to Article 3.1, the convention refers explicitly to the best interests of the child in Articles 9 (separation of the child from his or her parents), 10 (family reunification), 18 (parental responsibility), 20 (placement and special protection), 21 (adoption), 37.c (detention of minors) and 40, paragraph 2.b (juvenile justice). Therefore, it also seems appropriate to pay particular attention to the best interests of the child in family matters.

Even though each situation is unique, there are those where the best interests of the child deserve special attention. An example is divorce. The parents are sometimes so focused on their mutual fighting that they fail to assume their "parental responsibility". These situations can escalate to such an extent that external actors (social workers or judges specialised in juvenile affairs) have to intervene in the best interests of the child.

In the case of child abuse in the home environment, there is a risk of conflict between ensuring the child's safety and maintaining the child's relationship with the parents, in other words a choice between removal of residence or family therapy. It also needs to be considered whether any other alternatives can be taken in the best interests of the child. Another problematic situation is related to imprisonment. How should we deal with children when one of their parents is in prison? Is visiting an imprisoned parent in the best interests of the child? Is it also the case if the parent concerned has been convicted of sexual abuse? A child's right to know his or her origins cannot be discussed without referring to the best interests of the child. The number of children born into our modern society owing their birth to new fertility techniques is increasing steadily. Adopted children are looking for their roots, some of them for the culture and the habits of their country of origin. The rights of the children who want to know and those of the biological parents who want to remain unknown collide. All these situations are difficult and tricky, nevertheless they are very important and therefore they deserve a fundamental discussion.

Speech by Sven Gatz, Flemish Minister for Culture, Media, Youth and Brussels Affairs, Belgium

On 13 November 2014, Belgium took over the chairmanship of the Council of Europe Committee of Ministers. This was exactly one week before the 25th anniversary of the United Nations Convention on the Rights of the Child (UNCRC). It was a concurrence of circumstances which Belgium wanted to avail itself of to emphasise the role of children's rights in the European agenda. The Flemish and French Communities and the Federal Public Service "Justice" of Belgium decided to join forces in putting the best interests of the child on the agenda of the Belgian Chairmanship and to organise a conference on the best interests of the child. It was a natural choice to organise the conference in collaboration with the Council of Europe.

The decision to address children's rights came about long before the conference. In the autumn of 2012, three Belgian members of the Council of Europe Network of Children's Rights Co-ordinators resolved not to let the concurrence of the chairmanship and the anniversary of the UNCRC go by unnoticed. It was clearly agreed from the outset, however, that the intention could not be to just organise a festive celebration, as if there were no more problems with the application and implementation of the Convention on the Rights of the Child in Belgium and Europe in general. In fact, nothing is further from the truth. Many challenges are still left to be addressed.

Why, then, focus specifically on the best interests of the child? The concept of the best interests of the child is a frequently used and important, yet very vague, concept. The concept is so indeterminate that there is a danger of anyone working with children or developing policy with respect to children interpreting it in their own way. It was therefore important that the Committee on the Rights of the Child should offer more specific guidelines on how the concept should be interpreted and how it interacts with children's human rights. It did so by publishing in 2013 its General Comment No. 14 on the right of the child to have his or her best interests taken as a primary consideration (Article 3.1).

I would like to emphasise Flanders' commitment in the field of children's rights. Since 1997, Flanders has used two legally anchored pillars for monitoring compliance with the Convention on the Rights of the Child. The first is an independent pillar operated by the Flemish Parliament, namely the Flemish Office of the Children's Rights Commissioner. This office uses the resources it receives directly from the parliament to monitor compliance with children's rights standards. In addition, it deals with any complaints about violations of children's rights.

The second is the governmental pillar. Again since 1997, Flanders has conducted a co-ordinated children's rights policy. This policy focuses on the implementation of the Convention on the Rights of the Child and the concluding observations of the Committee on the Rights of the Child in the different Government of Flanders policy areas, always in consultation with civil society. At the Flemish level this is done within the framework of an integrated youth and children's rights policy. The Government of Flanders wants to continue the change of mindset which the Convention on the Rights of the Child brought about by giving an important place to children's participation rights. The autonomy of minors, which is indeed very specific to the Convention on the Rights of the Child, is highlighted even more, because the protection angle is less explicit in general human rights treaties.

Allow me to remind you of a relevant quote by Ms Maud de Boer-Buquicchio, former Deputy Secretary General of the Council of Europe and currently UN Special Rapporteur on the sale of children, child prostitution and child pornography: "Children are not mini-persons with mini-rights, mini-feelings and mini-human dignity. They are vulnerable human beings with full rights which require more, not less protection."[227] This brings us to the key question of this conference. What is the relation between the child's best interests and his or her rights, as guaranteed by the Convention on the Rights of the Child? The General Comment by the Committee on the Rights of the Child strongly focuses on the inter-relation between the two. However, practice is often very different from theory. In practice, we find that a lot of professionals use the child's best interests to justify decisions they take with respect to children, without even for a moment considering the rights of the child concerned. Are the best interests of the child a Trojan horse that has been smuggled into the Convention on the Rights of the Child? There seems to be a danger of best interests undermining the rights that are guaranteed for children by the convention. That is why we asked the Children's Rights Knowledge Centre (KeKi) to carry out a study in order to map tensions caused by the concept of the "child's best interests", using international examples.[228]

The Convention on the Rights of the Child is revolutionary in the sense that its Article 12 recognises children's participation rights. A child has the right to express his or her views freely and to have them given due weight in all matters affecting him or her. This means the child's views are essential in determining his or her best interests. Consequently, it can never be in the child's best interests for him or her not to be heard.

There are many open questions related to the concept of the best interests of the child. How do one child's best interests relate to another child's best interests? How do the best interests of individual children or a group of children relate to the best interests of other individuals or groups of individuals in society? It should be noted in this context that the concept of "best interests" features solely in relation to children.

---

227. Speech by Maud de Boer-Buquicchio at a conference on violence against children in Europe on 20 October 2005 in Berlin, http://crinarchive.org/resources/infoDetail.asp?ID=6407.
228. A summary of the study is included in this publication, see Chapter 1.6.

Other human rights treaties do not use any similar concept to describe potential best interests of other individuals.

The challenge we now face is to translate the theory of the convention and General Comment No. 14 into the practice of professionals and vice versa. I hope this conference will serve as a milestone and participate in a process where theory and practice come together in the child's best interests.

Speech by Rudy Demotte, Minister-President of the Wallonia-Brussels Federation Government in charge of Children's Rights, Belgium

Nelson Mandela once said: "There can be no keener revelation of a society's soul than the way in which it treats its children." And he was right. Children are one third of mankind, 2.2 billion human beings. But for some, as Urszula Markowska-Manista rightly points out in her text, "it is impossible to be a child".[229]

None of the rights of children withstands the trial of poverty. Social and economic inequalities impair children's potential and talents and prevent their development and emancipation. Children's socio-economic situations vary greatly throughout the Council of Europe region. In Belgium, almost one child in five lives at risk of poverty or social exclusion.[230] That is the principal challenge of the Belgian Governments, each according to its institutional purview.

At the level of the Wallonia-Brussels Federation, the fight against social inequalities and discrimination was one of the priorities of the three-year plan on children's rights for the period from 2011 to 2014. This aspect is taken up again in the 2015-2017 three-year plan adopted in March 2015 by the government.

These plans, which have been established for several years, correspond to a concerted strategy on children's rights. We are mobilising all ministers across the political spectrum so that they each take their share of responsibility in the protection, observance and attainment of children's rights. Acting in the child's best interests necessitates making the reduction of children's inequalities a priority at all times and especially in times of crisis.

Despite all the efforts already made, much remains for us to do. Democracy, the concept of rule of law and human rights, including the rights of the child, are values requiring constant vigilance. Whether in the world's most troubled regions or in Europe itself, our commitment to uphold these values must be complete.

Initiating the European Conference on the Best Interests of the Child, and making it one of the major events of the Belgian Chairmanship of the Council of Europe, were a priority in this context. How can we advance the situation of children? How do we narrow the gap between legal norms and the wishes of children, their day-to-day realities, their needs, their well-being here and now? When the question is tough,

229. See Chapter 2.1.
230. Eurostat, social inclusion statistics (2014). "At risk of poverty or social exclusion" is an indicator developed by Eurostat.

the answer must no doubt be bold and at the very least brave. The conference was the occasion for Belgium to reassert its ongoing commitment to children in the realisation of their rights as well as in the defence of their interests. For Belgium, the Council of Europe constitutes an essential institution for thought and action in the advancement of human rights.

The principle of the child's best interests is one of the four guiding principles of the Convention on the Rights of the Child, and yet this principle is but too seldom stated. Indeed, it seemed to us essential to place the child's interests, and specifically the interests of the most vulnerable children, at the centre of our adult concerns.

In 2008, the then Council of Europe Commissioner for Human Rights, Mr Thomas Hammarberg, uttered harsh but true words about the use of the concept of the child's best interests. I particularly recall this sentence perfectly encapsulating the state of mind that gave rise to our conference: "Excuses for violations of children's rights are clearly not what the principle of the best interests is about."[231]

Regarding the methodological approach, it was essential to conform to a holistic procedure that was necessarily multidisciplinary. The contradictions of diagnosis between theorists and practitioners (jurists, psychologists, social workers, educators) need to be overcome. They should work hand in hand at assessing, seeking and determining what is best for the child, specifically and tangibly. Joining together the theorists and the practitioners is clearly an avenue to be favoured for reducing the gap between adults' rules and intentions and children's life realities.

Several themes were proposed for discussion during this conference. First of all, one of the most important issues is the relationship between the child's best interests and his or her right to be heard. In practice, this relationship is often problematic. The challenge is significant as it queries our ability to accept that the word of children, their testimonies on their own experience, their expertise, are not only valid but above all productive. It is therefore imperative to respond positively to the challenges raised by involving children in the definition of their own interests. It does not suffice to hear children; we must listen to what they say in all circumstances!

Next, conflicts can occur between the child's best interests and the interests of the other parties involved. These other parties may be found in the child's personal circle – parents, sisters and brothers, family in the broad sense – or at the societal level. Several approaches and methodologies are possible to achieve this balance of interests. Children must carry more weight in the balancing of interests to tip the scales the right way.

It must also be possible to determine the child's best interests more effectively. Our decisions and actions must be underpinned by an evaluation of these interests in all facets, while defending an imperative of participation. Here I must note the originality of Bulgaria which, subsuming some of the criteria mentioned by the Committee on the Rights of the Child, is explicitly writing into its legislation the need to make an assessment of the child's interests.

---

231. Hammarberg T., "The principle of the best interests of the child – what it means and what it demands from adults", Speech given in Warsaw, 30 May 2008.

However, I must stress the difficulty of compiling practical tools to assess the child's interests. Here there is a deficiency to be compensated, a margin of progress for each of us. Any work in that respect by the Council of Europe, a master at collecting and disseminating good practices, can certainly be an asset.

Finally, mention should be made of the child's best interests in family litigation. Here we are no doubt at the core of the preoccupations of children themselves. The family is at once the source of life, a factor and a mainstay of children's well-being. Families today are reconstituted, single-parent, homoparental, conjugal and manifold other designations.

Three essential elements have caught my attention in the context of family litigation. The first concerns children with separated parents, an important reality in Belgium, the rate of separation being very high. If I were to formulate a single priority, I would say that we must endeavour to develop still further, alongside the judicial procedures, tools of a non-legal nature such as mediation which are particularly suitable and adequate for children.

The second essential element which I note concerns the temporary or lasting removal of children from the setting where they live. We should conscientiously and rigorously assess the direct and indirect impact in the short and long term of a decision on placement in a foster family or an institution. We must take into account the child's evolving characteristics and capabilities, the characteristics and capabilities of the family, and we must always envisage measures which can be reviewed and revised periodically. No decision of this type, which may potentially do severe harm to the tie between a child and its parent, can in fact be consistent with the child's interests if it is final, irrevocable and irreversible.

The European Conference on the Best Interests of the Child was just the starting point of our work. We have brought the results of our work to the attention of the Committee of Ministers of the Council of Europe, and it has taken note of our conclusions. The Committee of Ministers has also invited the Committee of Experts on the Council of Europe Strategy for the Rights of the Child (2016-2019) to take account of them in preparing its work. For our part, we shall continue tirelessly gathering the opinions of children in order to take informed political decisions.

Our results bear witness to our common determination to continue on the path travelled towards establishing a set of measures aimed at ensuring that children fully enjoy their rights. I greatly appreciated the wealth and the frankness of the viewpoints shared at the conference, the soundness of the field experiences mentioned, the determination expressed by all to look for solutions meeting the wishes and interests of children, all children. I would warmly thank all those who have contributed directly or indirectly to the conference and the publication.

Speech by Torbjørn Frøysnes, Ambassador, Head of the Council of Europe Liaison Office to the European Union

These are difficult and dangerous times in Europe. It is all the more commendable that Belgium, holding the Chair of the Committee of Ministers of the Council of Europe, while addressing the imminent conflict and foreign policy issues in Europe, also had the courage and capacity to address the important issue of the rights and interests of the child.

In 2014, we celebrated the 25th anniversary of the United Nations Convention on the Rights of the Child (UNCRC). It was a year where we had the duty to progress and not to regress. After the celebrations we still have that duty. So I would like to thank, most wholeheartedly, the Government of Belgium and the Flemish as well the French-speaking communities for the initiative of organising the European Conference on the Best Interests of the Child, and the ministers personally for their input for the conference and for this publication.

Children do not have well-funded lobbyists to speak for them in Brussels, like big corporations and the powerful interest organisations have. Adults can speak for themselves, but they also have to speak for children. Therefore, the initiative to hold a conference on the best interests of the child was all the more laudable. The conference gave children and their rights great attention – the attention of a large conference involving all relevant stakeholders working for a thorough reflection on children's best interests.

The concept of the best interests of the child was enshrined in the UNCRC in 1989. The convention aims at recognition of children as fully fledged bearers of a range of human rights, just like adults. It is still the most important international text for the protection of children's rights globally. Yet, has the concept of the best interests of the child been properly understood? Is it being applied in the way the drafters of the convention had in mind? Is it being applied in the way children themselves would like it to be used? Do we actually know how to apply it? These, and many more, important questions are addressed in this publication.

There are 150 million children living in the 47 member states of the Council of Europe. When the 10 founding member countries established the Council of Europe in 1949, the principles they agreed for this co-operation were the respect for human rights, democracy and rule of law. The European Convention on Human Rights (ETS No. 5, the Convention) that came into force in 1950 and has been ratified by all the member states of the Council of Europe guarantees the protection of human rights within the jurisdiction of the member states, also for children. As a founding member of the Council of Europe in 1949 and a co-author of the European Convention on Human Rights in 1950, Belgium has maintained a long and fine tradition right up to this conference as a protector and champion of human rights in Europe.

The Council of Europe considers the best interests of the child to be a fundamental underlying principle in all actions concerning children. In order to effectively safeguard the rights of children we need to act in their best interests. These two aims – promoting human rights and best interests – should not be mutually exclusive, quite the opposite. Although the European Convention on Human Rights does not contain the principle of the best interests of the child in its text, the European Court of Human Rights has interpreted the Convention in line with the UNCRC, so as to render it an underlying principle of the Convention. It is now referenced in many cases relating to children, and the Court has stated on many occasions that the best interests of the child must be a primary consideration in all actions concerning children.

The European Committee on Social Rights, which decides on complaints based on the revised European Social Charter (ETS No. 163, the Charter), has also interpreted the Charter in line with the principle of the best interests of the child despite the Charter being silent on this concept. The Committee now takes the principle into account when examining issues relating to children's rights. On the basis of this principle it has even extended some of the rights contained in the Charter to children in an irregular situation, that is irregular immigrants.

The various intergovernmental and expert committees of the Council of Europe have also contributed to the development of this principle through standard setting and monitoring. It is through these methods that the Council of Europe gives its member states guidance on what the principle implies in practice. Guidance is particularly important as the abstract nature of the principle lends itself to various interpretations that may in fact have a detrimental impact on children.

Several bodies of the Council of Europe work on children's rights and are actively engaged in further developing and safeguarding the best interests of the child. In addition to the European Court of Human Rights and the European Committee on Social Rights, these bodies include the Commissioner for Human Rights, the Parliamentary Assembly, the Venice Commission, the European Committee for the Prevention of Torture and Inhuman and Degrading Treatment or Punishment (CPT), the Group of Experts on Action against Trafficking in Human Beings (GRETA), the European Commission against Racism and Intolerance (ECRI) and the Committee of the Parties to the Convention on the Protection of Children against Sexual Exploitation and Sexual Abuse (Lanzarote Committee).

There are several challenges related to the application of the best interests of the child in practice. Children's interests may conflict with those of others – of other children, adults or the society. Many of the family law cases that are heard by the European Court of Human Rights are exactly about the conflict of those interests. However complex the assessment of children's best interests may be, I am convinced that we should always start with a respectful approach towards the child. And being respectful means first and foremost to listen attentively. Therefore, when talking about children's best interests, it is important to give children a say in an appropriate way. The Council of Europe provides guidance on this matter through its Recommendation CM/Rec(2012)2 from the Committee of Ministers to member States on participation of children and young people under the age of 18, as well as an assessment tool on participation.[232]

On a more political level, I think we can make some very clear statements on what is in the best interests of the child and what is not. First, we must consider the issue of irregular immigration that Europe is facing at the moment. Many countries still put children in immigration detention; such detention is clearly not in the best interests of the child and cannot be justified under any circumstances. Another clear issue is statelessness of children. As the Commissioner for Human Rights of the Council of Europe put it, it is in the best interests of the child to have citizenship from birth.

---

232. Council of Europe (2015), Child Participation Assessment Tool.

All children should be granted citizenship automatically at birth, even when their parents are stateless, because this is key to enjoying fully all human rights.[233]

The Council of Europe stands strong to protect human rights, and these include the human rights of children. Human rights and more so the interpretation of human rights are not carved in stone. Human rights are evolving, and so are children's rights. I hope that this publication will contribute to a better understanding of these rights. I also hope that the conference and this publication succeed in making a valuable contribution to the evolution of how we understand the child's right to have his or her best interests taken as a primary consideration.

233. Council of Europe Commissioner for Human Rights (2013), "Estonia: All children should be citizens".

Appendix II – Conclusions of the European Conference on the Best Interests of the Child within the framework of the 25th anniversary of the United Nations Convention on the Rights of the Child
(Brussels, 9-10 December 2014)[234]

Conclusions

"In all actions concerning children, whether undertaken by public or private social welfare institutions, courts of law, administrative authorities or legislative bodies, the best interests of the child shall be a primary consideration."

UNCRC, Art. 3, para. 1

On 9 and 10 December 2014 the Belgian authorities, in co-operation with the Children's Rights Division of the Council of Europe, organised the European Conference on the "Best Interests of the Child" in Brussels. The Conference, which permitted a dialogue between theory and practice, was organised within the framework of the Belgian Chairmanship of the Committee of Ministers of the Council of Europe in the perspective of strengthening human rights protection. This event celebrated, at the same time, the 25th anniversary of the United Nations Convention on the Rights of the Child (UNCRC).

The Conference pursued three objectives:

1. to take stock of the understanding and application of the child's best interests in the international context as well as in the various national contexts;

----

234. See document DD(2015)266E, distributed at the request of the Belgian Chair of the Ministers' Deputies on 31 March 2015.

2. to identify factors that hinder and those that drive as observed by decision makers in the application of the child's best interests and to outline solutions;

3. to find and develop ethical, procedural and practical standards which support practitioners and policy makers when they take into consideration the child's best interests.

Belgium considers that all objectives of the Conference have been accomplished.

The first day of the Conference focused on different perspectives on the child's best interests in general and the second day on the child's best interests in family matters. For Belgium, as well as for the Council of Europe, it was essential that experts, decision makers, practitioners, but also children could contribute to the discussions at the Conference and share their points of view. We would like to thank all those who were involved in this event. We hope that the Conference will contribute to a further enhancement of the position of children and their rights in all member States of the Council of Europe.

For Belgium the key messages of the Conference were the following:

- The Conference recalled the importance of Article 3, para 1 of the UNCRC and General Comment No. 14 (2013) on the right of the child to have his or her best interests taken as a primary consideration. The UN Committee on the Rights of the Child has pointed out that "an adult's judgment of a child's best interests cannot override the obligation to respect all the child's rights under the Convention."[235] There is no hierarchy of rights in the Convention; all the rights provided for therein are in the "child's best interests" and no right could be compromised by a negative interpretation of the child's best interests.[236]

- Article 12 of the UNCRC on children's participation is complementary to the best interests principle. The views of all children, including of those who are invisible and marginalised, and taking into account their evolving capacities (Art. 5 UNCRC), are an integral part of the assessment and determination process of the best interests of the child. Therefore children must have access to appropriate information (Art. 17 UNCRC). The new Optional Protocol to the UNCRC establishing a communications procedure was considered relevant in this context as a way to strengthen children's access to justice and their participation in the determination of their best interests.

- The concept of the best interests of the child is broad and vague and thus risks being used to justify decisions that run contrary to the rights of the child. Therefore, the assessment and determination of the child's best interests must be made on a case by case basis and founded on objective criteria. The non-exhaustive and non-hierarchical list of elements suggested in General Comment No. 14 (2013) should be considered in the determination of the best interest of the child. Furthermore, all, even political, decisions affecting children should be made on the basis of a child-rights impact assessment.

235. General Comment No. 13 (2011) on the right to protection from all forms of violence, para. 61.
236. General Comment No. 14 (2013) on the right of the child to have his or her best interests taken as a primary consideration (art. 3, para. 1), para. 4.

Children's interests should indeed be paramount and not just one of several considerations in decisions affecting children.

- In addition to an assessment of the best interests of the child at the moment a decision is taken, decisions affecting children should also be subject to independent monitoring to ensure that the best interests of the child serve as guiding principle also in the implementation of decisions.
- Both parents have the joint primary responsibility to bring up their children. The relationship between children and their parents is considered to be highly important. The Conference showed that this relationship can be subject to severe tensions, e.g. due to the imprisonment of one of the parents, divorce of the parents, child maltreatment, the child's removal from the family or when children are insecure about their origins such as in the case of adoption or conception through medically assisted reproduction. In such situations, it is important to assess and determine the best interests of the child in a way that the ties with both parents and other significant family members can be maintained while ensuring that the child has the opportunity to fully develop his or her potential.
- To safeguard the application of the best interests of the child principle in practice, member States need to ensure training of all professions involved in decisions for and with children: judges, lawyers, social workers, educators, teachers etc. Member States should also support parents in a way that they can fulfil their responsibility for the upbringing and development of the child.

By this way Belgium wants to thank the Secretariat of the Council of Europe and especially the Children's Rights Division of the Council of Europe, for its involvement and constructive support in the organisation of the Conference. Belgium hopes that the results of the Conference will strengthen the position of children and their rights in the member States of the Council of Europe. Therefore, Belgium would welcome, in co-operation with the Secretariat, to publish all expert contributions to the Conference by the end of this year.

Appendix III – Executive summaries of the contributions

Chapter 1 – The concept of the best interests of the child: general reflections

Jorge Cardona Llorens presents the Committee on the Rights of the Child's General Comment No. 14 (2013) on the right of the child to have his or her interests taken as a primary consideration. Cardona discusses the drafting of the General Comment as well as its strengths and weaknesses. He concentrates on four main questions. First, best interests constitute an indeterminate but not discretionary legal concept, and their assessment and determination should be founded on objective criteria. General Comment No. 14 proposes a list of criteria to be applied in the determination of best interests. Second, Cardona Llorens addresses the problems of assessing and determining children's best interests in the adoption of general measures, such as legislation and policy making. The Committee on the Rights of the Child recommends the use of child-rights impact assessments in decision making. Third, he analyses the relationship between the child's best interests and other legitimate interests involved. Conflicts between a child's best interests and other interests or rights have to be solved on a case-by-case basis. In some situations, such as adoption, the best interests of the child have to be "the" instead of "a" primary consideration. Lastly, the author discusses the threefold legal nature of the child's best interests as an interpretive legal principle, a subjective right and a procedural rule. According to Cardona, the threefold nature of the best interests concept is key to understanding the committee's perception of the child's best interests.

Nigel Cantwell provides a critical analysis of the concept of the best interests of the child. He points out that the concept existed long before children were granted human rights, and it has in fact often been misused to justify actions that violate children's rights. According to Cantwell, the prominent role assigned to the concept is mistaken and even dangerous in a context where children have human rights. The implications of applying the concept in the way foreseen by the United Nations Convention on the Rights of the Child (UNCRC) have not been thought through or addressed in a sufficiently critical manner. In international law, Cantwell notes, the best interests concept is used solely in relation to children. In the drafting of the UNCRC, the concept suddenly broadened in scope, and the implications of this were not properly discussed. The elevation of best interests to one of the general principles of the UNCRC was unfounded, as the Committee on the Rights of the Child is not in a position to elevate some articles above others; General Comment No. 14 does not sufficiently explain the special role of best interests. Intercountry adoption is an example of how best interests can pose problems as a paramount consideration, one that is at the same time hard to determine. Cantwell does identify positive contributions of best interests, however; he argues that the concept functions best when it is used in situations where rights considerations alone do not provide sufficient guidance or grounds for decision making. Best interests should play a role only when necessary, appropriate and feasible as a tool for advancing the human rights of children.

Olga Khazova discusses challenges in interpreting and applying the concept of the best interests of the child. She introduces problems related to the concept, such as practical difficulties in applying it. These include determining what is in the best interests of the child, striking a balance between different interests, and deciding on the factors that should be taken into account. As there is no comprehensive definition of best interests, the concept has been subject to criticism; it is vague, but also flexible. However, the principles of best interests and that of welfare have to be distinguished from each other. General Comment No. 14, Khazova argues, will advance a proper application of the best interests concept. This has been difficult, particularly in family-related cases. First, in custody disputes in cases of divorce or parental separation, it is necessary to ensure that the child can maintain close contact with both parents. Second, poverty, bad housing and a poor environment are not in the best interests of any child. According to the jurisprudence of the European Court of Human Rights this does not, however, mean that the children should be separated from their parents. Third, the concept of the best interests of the child in the context of what is sometimes called "alternative families" is an evolving issue in Europe. Fourth, a child's right to know his or her origins has to be respected. Fifth, there are procedural issues that need attention. Child participation has to be promoted and professionals appropriately trained.

Gerison Lansdown observes that the best interests principle can be misused, which is why the Committee on the Rights of the Child issued General Comment No. 14. Lansdown mentions two central issues in the interpretation of the best interests principle: first, no action can be justified as being in a child's best interests if it serves to violate their rights; second, it is important to adopt a holistic approach to the realisation of children's rights. Additionally, the determination of best interests must take account of the views of the child. According to Lansdown, evolving capacities, the views of the child and substantive UNCRC rights are key components in determining best interests. Article 5 of the UNCRC on the evolving capacities of the child provides the transitional linkage between the initial dependency of a newborn child and the full autonomy afforded to an adult. Article 12 complements Article 5 by asserting that in all matters affecting children, they have a right to express their views and have them taken seriously. Many other rights in the UNCRC are more effectively realised if the child's right to be heard informs their implementation. In health care as well as in the field of child protection, for example, children's interests are best served if their voices are heard. Lansdown argues that risk of misapplication of the best interests principle arises when it is regarded as a stand-alone principle, or as a trump to override all other perspectives. The principle must be applied through the lens of the UNCRC as a whole, and determined with respect for children's own views and for their right to take increasing responsibility for decisions in accordance with their evolving capacities.

Jacques Fierens compares the best interests principle to the North Star. The principle is difficult to grasp but can fulfil its function in countless situations. The best interests principle is, inevitably, undefinable in a theoretical sense: it obtains its meaning in relation to particular situations. The principle is likened to a compass that does not in itself tell us what the answer is; rather, it indicates a direction. Conflicts between the best interests of the child and other interests are not always what they seem, as the perspective of the observer affects the situation. Sometimes best interests are trumped on unsatisfactory grounds. In defining the best interests of the child, hearing the child is essential. "Respect due to the child", Fierens suggests, is preferable to "best interests". The concept existed before the UNCRC and is part of a broader movement towards acknowledging children's rights, and the respect they should be accorded.

Eveline van Hooijdonk discusses a report by the Children's Rights Knowledge Centre (KeKi) on common points of tension in the translation of the principle of the best interests of the child from theory to practice. KeKi found four areas of tension: the workability of the best interests principle in practical situations; conflicts of interest; the instrumental view of participation; and in protecting children's best interests on a policy level. The KeKi study showed that practitioners worldwide are not discouraged by theoretical difficulties and the vagueness of the best interests principle. There are creative ways to effectively use this concept in different professional situations. It is important to invest in child-specific training programmes for professionals as well as in monitoring, feedback and ex-post evaluation. Children's interests should be clearly distinguished from other parties' interests, and children's meaningful participation in decisions affecting them should be a priority both for individual and collective decisions. Child-rights impact assessments, for instance, can provide inspiration for best interests assessments.

Chapter 2 – Assessing, determining and monitoring best interests

Urszula Markowska-Manista discusses the practical involvement of children in their rights, as articulated by the well-known Polish-Jewish doctor, pedagogue and social activist Janusz Korczak. She focuses in particular on his theories with regards to emancipation, and integrates his principles into the analysis of research on children's everyday lives. In exploring how marginalised children could be involved in the determination of their own best interests, the pedagogy of, Korczak is drawn on, based as they are on respect towards children and letting them play an active role in their own lives.

Margrite Kalverboer introduces a method for assessing and determining the best interests of the child. The theoretical framework presented can be used in decision-making procedures in different (legal) situations where a child might be involved. The article presents the separate pedagogy used, that of child psychology, as well as the concept of the best interests of the child from a combined child development and children's rights perspective. It also introduces the Best Interests of the Child model (BIC model), which consists of 14 child-rearing conditions in a child's life that must be of sufficiently high quality to enable a good childhood and safeguard child development. The high quality of these factors is in the best interests of the child. In this regard the BIC questionnaire, an interdisciplinary tool to assess the child's best interests on the basis of combined pedagogical, child development and legal principles, can be employed. General Comment No. 14 from the Committee on the Rights of the Child is also discussed.

Carla van Os discusses applying the BIC model presented by Margrite Kalverboer to refugee children, addressing factors that should be accounted for while making the first decision in the migration procedure. Newly arrived refugee children face many challenges that underline the necessity of a good best interests assessment. Decisions about the child's need for international protection should be based on the child's right to development, in a similar way to how the right to development is applied in child protection law. Particularly for recently arrived refugee children, it is necessary to assess whether their development was endangered before they fled and, if so, whether the conditions for development are likely to improve in case the child returns.

Hanne op de Beeck discusses the monitoring of best interests decision making. The most extensive monitoring initiatives regarding best-interests decisions have been developed in the domain of migration. Monitoring systems for return decisions can serve as a model for other best-interests decisions. The article suggests that the duty of states to mainstream the best interests principle in different policy domains, such as migration should be included in Article 3 of the UNCRC. It appears that at least the responsibility for establishing a monitoring system lies with the states. For return decisions, the situation is not clear, though the receiving state may be said to bear this responsibility. Another important concern is the implementation of the monitoring process. First, the intrinsic motivation of the states should be addressed. The second option would be to enforce qualitative monitoring and evaluation by states. A third option would be to create a mixed model in which states and non-governmental organisations carry out the monitoring together through a complementary system. In addition to these possibilities, media should be engaged and data collection and registration systems improved. As the concept of the best interests of the child is a dynamic one, establishing dynamic decision-making processes is important. Monitoring and evaluation can add to such a dynamic process.

Chapter 3 – Best interests of the child in different environments

Regína Jensdóttir discusses the difficulties surrounding the overall concept of the best interest of the child from the perspective of the Council of Europe. According to Jensdottir, there is a need to understand and implement the best interest as a guiding principle and not as a static definition. Defining it would actually weaken its role and overall impact on children's lives. By analysing the Council of Europe's bodies and work, Jensdóttir demonstrates how the best interest can be used and developed as an underlying principle and as a guide, therefore guaranteeing a stronger safeguard of children's rights in general. Three functions served by the principle of the best interest are presented, namely to combine rights, to balance rights and to guide the implementation of these rights. It is by understanding and taking into account these three guiding functions, that the best interest of a child will be determined in practice.

Margaret Tuite writes about the concept of the best interests of the child in the work of the European Union. The concept is embedded in several pieces of EU legislation, such as Article 24 of the Charter of Fundamental Rights and the Brussels IIa Regulation covering cross-border family conflicts. A report on the application of Brussels IIa, published in 2014, concluded that targeted improvements to the existing rules are needed. An EU study to collect data on children's involvement in criminal, civil and administrative judicial proceedings also sought to investigate how member states of the EU advance or promote best interests as a principle, a right and a rule of procedure. The study revealed differences among states and showed that measures to ensure the effective implementation of the best interests of the child in judicial proceedings are more strongly developed in the areas of family disputes and placement into care than in other areas of law. Some countries may not apply such measures to asylum and immigration law, for example. This is highly problematic, as the best interests of the child must be a primary consideration in all cases concerning children.

Tam Baillie provides two perspectives regarding the application of the best interests of the child principle: first, the application of best interests at a population level, and second, the application for individual children. Applying the best interests principle at a population level is challenging with regards to economic, social and cultural rights, as there is no redress when economic policies fail to take account of children's best interests. There are several challenges related to application in individual situations as well, such as conflicts between maximising the development of the child and the harm caused by removing the child from the family. Choosing suitable means for adequately implementing the best interests of the child can be equally problematic, as are situations of domestic abuse.

Johanna Nyman analyses the best interests concept from the point of view of young people's rights. She underlines participation rights (Article 12, UNCRC) as one of the most important aspects of the principle of the best interests of the child. Participation is also one of the pillars of the work that the European Youth Forum conducts. According to Nyman, the most effective way to encourage child and youth participation is through representative, democratic organisations. Young people should be able to participate in society. However, the level of participation of a child always needs to be adapted to his or her evolving capacities. The Optional Protocol to the Convention on the Rights of the Child on a communications procedure has opened up new possibilities for children to participate in decisions affecting them. But concern remains regarding young people aged 18 or older as they are excluded from the scope of the UNCRC. The transition from childhood to adulthood therefore needs attention. Research on young people's human rights as well as on the impact of policy measures on children and youth would be a good basis for investigating the differences between traditional youth and child policies.

Bernard De Vos discusses the best interests concept from the point of view of an ombudsman and distinguishes two ways to assess best interests: an abstract, general assessment that is valid for all children, and a realistic assessment of a very precise situation. De Vos concentrates on assessing best interests on a general level, and sees practical engagement as essential in promoting best interests. The manipulation of best interests for the wrong purposes has to be stopped, and the importance of hearing children when defining their best interests is crucial. Several ethical questions to which new technologies contribute are introduced, such as allowing euthanasia for children, and assisted reproduction.

Jana Hainsworth describes the challenges civil society faces in relation to best interests. Eurochild, as a civil society organisation, is concerned with lobbying for the best interests of the child, and using EU leverage to support better policies and investment at national level. Indeed, the concept of the best interests of the child can serve as a helpful tool for civil society in its efforts to protect children's rights. On the other hand, it can have damaging effects if misused. The concept of the best interests of the child can and should be used to mainstream the rights of the child in practical work. In this regard, a rights-based understanding of the best interests of the child is essential. Recently, there have been many positive developments at policy level, such as the European Parliament resolution on the 25th anniversary of the UNCRC, the establishment of an Intergroup on Children's Rights, the European Commission's Recommendation "Investing in children: breaking the cycle of disadvantage", and various children's rights-related activities by the Council of Europe. However, levels of child poverty and social exclusion are rising in Europe. Hainsworth considers it important that government representatives act to influence policy, practice and spending and promote children's rights more broadly. Without support from public authorities, civil society cannot work efficiently.

Chapter 4 – Best interests of the child in family affairs

Aida Grgić discusses the best interests of the child in the context of Article 8 of the European Convention on Human Rights. Even though the Convention is not a specialised children's rights convention and does not expressly refer to best interests, the European Court of Human Rights has referred to the concept on numerous occasions. Grgić systematically addresses cases related to custody and access rights, identity issues (paternity, maternity and surrogacy), placement in care, adoption, and child abduction. The Court has consistently acknowledged that the best interests of the child must be a primary consideration in all cases concerning children. It cannot develop a set of criteria specifying what constitutes the best interests that can be applied to every case, but it could in particular cases describe more clearly what it considers to be in the best interests of the child.

Cristina Martins discusses the best interests concept in the context of social work. Social workers have the responsibility to promote social justice. Common social work standards that respect human rights are essential, which is why the International

Federation of Social Workers (IFSW) is striving towards them in day-to-day professional practice. The IFSW trains social workers to take human rights into account in their daily work via training manuals and in 2002, it published a professional training manual on the UNCRC. Martins explains that when looking at children as a group, social workers can focus on organising different kinds of activities that benefit children, and she draws on her experience of working at the Oncology Paediatric Service in Portugal.

Valeriu Ghileţchi analyses the best interests of the child in removal decisions. The report "Social services in Europe: legislation and practice of the removal of children from their families in Council of Europe member states", produced by the Parliamentary Assembly of the Council of Europe, is discussed. The report found that national legislation in most countries of the Council of Europe complies with international law. The number of children taken into care varies widely from country to country, and though direct comparisons were not possible due to the ambiguity of the data available, some conclusions have been drawn. In some countries, social services take children into care too rashly, whereas in some countries, social services do not take children into care quickly enough, or return children to abusive or neglectful parental care. The recommendations the Parliamentary Assembly adopted, based on the report, are also discussed.

Astrid Hirschelmann addresses the issues that a child whose parent is imprisoned may face. The best interests of the child are central in this context, but not enough information is available on the topic. The project "Regards d'enfants sur l'incarceration: mise en place d'un groupe d'expression d'enfants de parents ou proches incarcérés (RESI)" (children's perspectives concerning imprisonment: setting up a self-expression group of children with imprisoned parents or loved ones) aimed at creating and testing a new support system in the form of a self-expression group intended for children with an imprisoned parent or close relative. The response from children was generally positive, though there were some limitations. The recommendations formulated at the end of the project emphasise the importance of a community-based approach to aid the families of imprisoned people.

Géraldine Mathieu discusses the child's best interests and the right to know his or her origins. The search for one's origins is a special question, as origins affect our personality and identity. The UNCRC secures for the child the right to know his or her parents, as far as possible (Article 7), and requires states to safeguard his or her identity (Article 8). These two articles, however, leave some room for interpretation to states. The Committee on the Rights of the Child has on various occasions recommended that states take measures so that children can, as far as possible, know the identity of their parents. Council of Europe member states should exercise their discretion in compliance with the obligations arising from the European Convention on Human Rights, especially Article 8, as its case law indicates that the interest of the individual in knowing his or her origins is fundamental but not absolute. However, this discretion remains large, and Mathieu suggests that the right to know one's origins should be expressly and clearly enshrined at the international level as well as in national constitutions even if it is not absolute.

Sales agents for publications of the Council of Europe
Agents de vente des publications du Conseil de l'Europe

BELGIUM/BELGIQUE
La Librairie Européenne -
The European Bookshop
Rue de l'Orme, 1
BE-1040 BRUXELLES
Tel.: +32 (0)2 231 04 35
Fax: +32 (0)2 735 08 60
E-mail: info@libeurop.eu
http://www.libeurop.be

Jean De Lannoy/DL Services
c/o Michot Warehouses
Bergense steenweg 77
Chaussée de Mons
BE-1600 SINT PIETERS LEEUW
Fax: +32 (0)2 706 52 27
E-mail: jean.de.lannoy@dl-servi.com
http://www.jean-de-lannoy.be

BOSNIA AND HERZEGOVINA/
BOSNIE-HERZÉGOVINE
Robert's Plus d.o.o.
Marka Maruliça 2/V
BA-71000 SARAJEVO
Tel.: + 387 33 640 818
Fax: + 387 33 640 818
E-mail: robertsplus@bih.net.ba

CANADA
Renouf Publishing Co. Ltd.
22-1010 Polytek Street
CDN-OTTAWA, ONT K1J 9J1
Tel.: +1 613 745 2665
Fax: +1 613 745 7660
Toll-Free Tel.: (866) 767-6766
E-mail: order.dept@renoufbooks.com
http://www.renoufbooks.com

CROATIA/CROATIE
Robert's Plus d.o.o.
Marasoviçeva 67
HR-21000 SPLIT
Tel.: + 385 21 315 800, 801, 802, 803
Fax: + 385 21 315 804
E-mail: robertsplus@robertsplus.hr

CZECH REPUBLIC/
RÉPUBLIQUE TCHÈQUE
Suweco CZ, s.r.o.
Klecakova 347
CZ-180 21 PRAHA 9
Tel.: +420 2 424 59 204
Fax: +420 2 848 21 646
E-mail: import@suweco.cz
http://www.suweco.cz

DENMARK/DANEMARK
GAD
Vimmelskaftet 32
DK-1161 KØBENHAVN K
Tel.: +45 77 66 60 00
Fax: +45 77 66 60 01
E-mail: reception@gad.dk
http://www.gad.dk

FINLAND/FINLANDE
Akateeminen Kirjakauppa
PO Box 128
Keskuskatu 1
FI-00100 HELSINKI
Tel.: +358 (0)9 121 4430
Fax: +358 (0)9 121 4242
E-mail: akatilaus@akateeminen.com
http://www.akateeminen.com

FRANCE
Please contact directly /
Merci de contacter directement
Council of Europe Publishing
Editions du Conseil de l'Europe
FR-67075 STRASBOURG cedex
Tel.: +33 (0)3 88 41 25 81
Fax: +33 (0)3 88 41 39 10
E-mail: publishing@coe.int
http://book.coe.int

Librairie Kléber
1 rue des Francs-Bourgeois
FR-67000 STRASBOURG
Tel.: +33 (0)3 88 15 78 88
Fax: +33 (0)3 88 15 78 80
E-mail: librairie-kleber@coe.int
http://www.librairie-kleber.com

GREECE/GRÈCE
Librairie Kauffmann s.a.
Stadiou 28
GR-105 64 ATHINAI
Tel.: +30 210 32 55 321
Fax.: +30 210 32 30 320
E-mail: ord@otenet.gr
http://www.kauffmann.gr

HUNGARY/HONGRIE
Euro Info Service
Pannónia u. 58.
PF. 1039
HU-1136 BUDAPEST
Tel.: +36 1 329 2170
Fax: +36 1 349 2053
E-mail: euroinfo@euroinfo.hu
http://www.euroinfo.hu

ITALY/ITALIE
Licosa SpA
Via Duca di Calabria, 1/1
IT-50125 FIRENZE
Tel.: +39 0556 483215
Fax: +39 0556 41257
E-mail: licosa@licosa.com
http://www.licosa.com

NORWAY/NORVÈGE
Akademika
Postboks 84 Blindern
NO-0314 OSLO
Tel.: +47 2 218 8100
Fax: +47 2 218 8103
E-mail: support@akademika.no
http://www.akademika.no

POLAND/POLOGNE
Ars Polona JSC
25 Obroncow Street
PL-03-933 WARSZAWA
Tel.: +48 (0)22 509 86 00
Fax: +48 (0)22 509 86 10
E-mail: arspolona@arspolona.com.pl
http://www.arspolona.com.pl

PORTUGAL
Marka Lda
Rua dos Correeiros 61-3
PT-1100-162 LISBOA
Tel: 351 21 3224040
Fax: 351 21 3224044
Web: www.marka.pt
E mail: apoio.clientes@marka.pt

RUSSIAN FEDERATION/
FÉDÉRATION DE RUSSIE
Ves Mir
17b, Butlerova ul. - Office 338
RU-117342 MOSCOW
Tel.: +7 495 739 0971
Fax: +7 495 739 0971
E-mail: orders@vesmirbooks.ru
http://www.vesmirbooks.ru

SWITZERLAND/SUISSE
Planetis Sàrl
16 chemin des Pins
CH-1273 ARZIER
Tel.: +41 22 366 51 77
Fax: +41 22 366 51 78
E-mail: info@planetis.ch

TAIWAN
Tycoon Information Inc.
5th Floor, No. 500, Chang-Chun Road
Taipei, Taiwan
Tel.: 886-2-8712 8886
Fax: 886-2-8712 4747, 8712 4777
E-mail: info@tycoon-info.com.tw
orders@tycoon-info.com.tw

UNITED KINGDOM/ROYAUME-UNI
The Stationery Office Ltd
PO Box 29
GB-NORWICH NR3 1GN
Tel.: +44 (0)870 600 5522
Fax: +44 (0)870 600 5533
E-mail: book.enquiries@tso.co.uk
http://www.tsoshop.co.uk

UNITED STATES and CANADA/
ÉTATS-UNIS et CANADA
Manhattan Publishing Co
670 White Plains Road
USA-10583 SCARSDALE, NY
Tel: + 1 914 472 4650
Fax: +1 914 472 4316
E-mail: coe@manhattanpublishing.com
http://www.manhattanpublishing.com

Council of Europe Publishing/Éditions du Conseil de l'Europe
FR-67075 STRASBOURG Cedex
Tel.: +33 (0)3 88 41 25 81 – Fax: +33 (0)3 88 41 39 10 – E-mail: publishing@coe.int – Website: http://book.coe.int